AF414613

Peppermint Perfection in Holiday Cookies

Peppermint Perfection: Candy Cane-Inspired Treats

Jessica Reynolds

© Copyright 2024 - All rights reserved.

The content contained within this book may not be reproduced, duplicated or transmitted without direct written permission from the author or the publisher.

Under no circumstances will any blame or legal responsibility be held against the publisher, or author, for any damages, reparation, or monetary loss due to the information contained within this book, either directly or indirectly.

Legal Notice:

This book is copyright protected. It is only for personal use. You cannot amend, distribute, sell, use, quote or paraphrase any part, or the content within this book, without the consent of the author or publisher.

Disclaimer Notice:

Please note the information contained within this document is for educational and entertainment purposes only. All effort has been executed to present accurate, up to date, reliable, complete information. No warranties of any kind are declared or implied. Readers acknowledge that the author is not engaging in the rendering of legal, financial, medical or professional advice. The content within this book has been derived from various sources. Please consult a licensed professional before attempting any techniques outlined in this book.

By reading this document, the reader agrees that under no circumstances is the author responsible for any losses, direct or indirect, that are incurred as a result of the use of information contained within this document, including, but not limited to, errors, omissions, or inaccuracies.

Table of Contents

INTRODUCTION

Step into the enchanting world of holiday baking, where the refreshing essence of peppermint takes center stage. Welcome to "Peppermint Perfection in Holiday Cookies - Candy Cane-Inspired Treats," an e-book that promises to elevate your seasonal baking experience with the delightful charm of peppermint. As the air fills with the sweet aroma of candy canes and festive cheer, this collection of recipes is crafted to immerse you in the joyous spirit of the holidays.

In this e-book, we embark on a journey beyond the ordinary, exploring peppermint's rich history and cultural significance in holiday traditions. From its origins to its evolution into a symbol of seasonal delight, we delve into the sweet affair between peppermint and holiday celebrations. Discover the fascinating connection between peppermint and candy canes, unraveling their history and the timeless charm they bring to our festive tables.

Our exploration extends to the heart of peppermint baking, introducing essential ingredients and tools that form the foundation for peppermint perfection. Whether you're a seasoned baker or a passionate novice, these chapters guide you through the key elements contributing to the irresistible allure of peppermint-infused treats.

The e-book unfolds with classic peppermint cookie recipes that evoke the nostalgia of holiday seasons past. From the simplicity of peppermint chocolate chip cookies to the intricacies of candy cane sugar cookies, these timeless classics lay the groundwork for the delectable journey ahead. But we don't stop there—brace yourself for an extravaganza of creative twists, pushing the boundaries of peppermint perfection with innovative treats that redefine holiday indulgence.

Venture further into gluten-free and vegan peppermint options, ensuring that the joy of peppermint-infused delights is accessible to all. Explore the art of perfecting peppermint decorations with a royal icing masterclass and creative tips for decorating your treats with a personal touch.

As we navigate through the pages of "Peppermint Perfection: Candy Cane-Inspired Treats," anticipate a celebration of health-conscious alternatives, peppermint treats for special occasions, and a heartfelt conclusion that encourages you to share your peppermint traditions. This e-book is more than a guide; it's an invitation to infuse your holiday season with the magic of peppermint and create moments of sweet perfection that will linger in the memories of family and friends for years to come.

CHAPTER I

A History of Peppermint in Holiday Baking

Origins of Peppermint in Culinary Use

The origins of peppermint in culinary use are deeply rooted in the annals of history, tracing back to ancient civilizations where the aromatic herb gained recognition for its unique flavor profile and therapeutic properties. Mentha × piperita, commonly known as peppermint, is a hybrid mint species cross between watermint (Mentha aquatica) and spearmint (Mentha spicata). Its distinct and invigorating taste and refreshing fragrance have made peppermint a staple in culinary traditions across various cultures.

Returning to ancient Egypt, peppermint found its place in the kitchen and the apothecary. The ancient Egyptians valued peppermint for its medicinal properties, using it in remedies to soothe digestive issues and alleviate headaches. Over time, this versatile herb entered culinary practices, enhancing the flavor of foods and beverages. The Greeks and Romans also recognized the value of peppermint, incorporating it into sweet and savory dishes.

Peppermint's journey through history took a notable turn during the Middle Ages when monasteries played a crucial role in preserving and disseminating knowledge about herbs and their uses. Monks cultivated and propagated peppermint, appreciating its culinary versatility. With its ability to add depth to dishes and its reputation for aiding digestion, peppermint became a prized ingredient in medieval European kitchens.

In the Renaissance era, peppermint continued to be a symbol of refinement in culinary arts. Its inclusion in recipes showcased the sophistication of a chef's repertoire. As exploration and trade routes expanded, peppermint found its way into diverse cuisines, each culture adapting it to suit their culinary preferences. In Asia, particularly in traditional Chinese medicine, peppermint was valued for its cooling properties and often used in medicinal and culinary applications.

The journey of peppermint in culinary use reached new heights during the 18th and 19th centuries. The emergence of peppermint extracts and oils revolutionized how the herb could be incorporated into recipes. This concentrated form allowed chefs and home cooks to precisely infuse peppermint flavor into their creations. The candy-making industry seized upon this development, giving rise to the iconic peppermint candies and sweets we now associate with holiday traditions.

The widespread availability of peppermint extracts paved the way for its incorporation into various culinary delights. From peppermint-infused chocolates and confections to beverages and desserts, the herb became synonymous with festive occasions and celebrations. Peppermint's crisp and cooling flavor contrasted with sweet and savory dishes, making it a versatile ingredient in the culinary landscape.

In the modern era, the use of peppermint in culinary creations has expanded beyond traditional boundaries. The global culinary scene embraces peppermint in diverse forms, from peppermint-flavored beverages to innovative desserts that showcase its versatility. Peppermint's popularity during the holiday season, particularly in the form of candy canes and seasonal treats, has become a cherished tradition in many households.

Furthermore, the recognition of peppermint's potential health benefits has contributed to its continued presence in kitchens worldwide. Beyond its delightful taste, peppermint is celebrated for its digestive properties and ability to add a refreshing note to various culinary concoctions. Health-conscious consumers often turn to peppermint-infused recipes as a flavorful way to support well-being.

In conclusion, the origins of peppermint in culinary use weave a rich tapestry that spans centuries and crosses cultural boundaries. Peppermint has evolved remarkably, from its early recognition for medicinal properties in ancient civilizations to its elevated status in contemporary kitchens. Today, as we savor the unmistakable taste of peppermint in holiday treats and year-round delights, we pay homage to a herb that has stood the test of time, enhancing our culinary experiences with its timeless and refreshing essence.

Evolution of Peppermint in Holiday Treats

The evolution of peppermint in holiday treats is a delightful journey that mirrors the changing tapestry of festive culinary traditions throughout the ages. With its refreshing flavor and aromatic charm, Peppermint has become synonymous with the holiday season, gracing tables with freshness and sweetness. Its presence in holiday treats can be traced back to ancient times when the herb's medicinal properties were revered, and its culinary potential began to unfold.

In the medieval era, monasteries were pivotal in cultivating and preserving knowledge about herbs, including peppermint. The herb found its way into holiday concoctions as monks appreciated its ability to enhance the taste and digestion of festive feasts. With its relaxed and refreshing notes, Peppermint became integral to holiday fare, offering a unique sensory experience during seasonal celebrations.

As the Renaissance era dawned, peppermint's status in culinary arts ascended. The advent of peppermint extracts and oils allowed chefs to infuse their holiday treats with a concentrated burst of minty goodness. This innovation gave rise to a spectrum of peppermint-flavored delights, from confections to beverages. The elegant allure of peppermint-laced desserts and candies became synonymous with refinement and celebration during the festive season.

The 18th and 19th centuries marked a transformative period for peppermint in holiday treats, particularly in the confectionery world. The widespread availability of peppermint extracts facilitated the creation of iconic holiday sweets, such as peppermint candies and candy canes. These treats symbolized the festive season with their distinctive red and white stripes. The confectionery industry seized upon peppermint's visual appeal and enchanting flavor, turning it into an integral part of holiday traditions worldwide.

The introduction of peppermint-flavored chocolates further enriched the holiday treat landscape. The marriage of rich, velvety chocolate with peppermint's crisp and cool notes created a symphony of flavors that captivated the taste buds. Peppermint bark, a classic holiday confection, was a testament to this harmonious pairing. Layers of dark or white chocolate infused with peppermint oil and crushed candy canes became a staple on holiday dessert tables, embodying the essence of festive indulgence.

In the 20th century, with the advent of mass production and global trade, peppermint treats became more accessible to a broader audience. The iconic candy cane, which originated in Germany, became a ubiquitous symbol of the holiday season. Its hook shape and distinctive red and white stripes captivated children and adults, making it a cherished tradition. Peppermint-flavored beverages, from hot cocoa to candy cane-infused cocktails, further solidified the herb's place in holiday celebrations.

The modern era witnesses a dynamic and creative exploration of peppermint in holiday treats. Artisanal bakers and home cooks alike embrace the versatility of peppermint, incorporating it into a myriad of desserts beyond traditional confections. Peppermint-flavored cookies, cakes, and ice creams grace holiday dessert tables, offering a contemporary twist on classic recipes. The rise of culinary innovation has given birth to unique peppermint-infused creations, pushing the boundaries of traditional holiday treats.

Moreover, the cultural exchange facilitated by globalization has led to the incorporation of peppermint into diverse holiday traditions. In some regions, peppermint is featured in traditional holiday dishes, adding a touch of minty freshness to time-honored recipes. This cross-cultural infusion of flavors contributes to the dynamic evolution of peppermint in holiday treats, as culinary enthusiasts draw inspiration from around the world.

Health-conscious consumers also embrace the festive allure of peppermint in their holiday treats. Peppermint's reputation for aiding digestion aligns with the spirit of indulgence that often accompanies holiday feasts. Peppermint tea and peppermint-infused desserts are a refreshing counterpoint to the richness of holiday fare, providing a sensory and digestive respite during the festive season.

In conclusion, the evolution of peppermint in holiday treats is a captivating narrative that spans centuries, weaving through the annals of culinary history and cultural traditions. From its early days as a medicinal herb to its transformation into a symbol of festive indulgence, peppermint has journeyed through time, leaving an indelible mark on holiday tables worldwide. Whether it's the iconic candy cane, the velvety richness of peppermint bark, or contemporary artisanal creations, peppermint continues to enchant and elevate the holiday treat experience, embodying the season's magic in every refreshing bite.

Cultural Significance of Peppermint in Different Traditions

The cultural significance of peppermint unfolds as a tapestry woven with threads of tradition, symbolism, and the aromatic charm of this versatile herb. Across diverse cultures and traditions, peppermint has found its place in culinary practices, medicinal remedies, and festive celebrations, becoming a symbol of refreshment, vitality, and seasonal joy.

In European traditions, peppermint emerges as a herald of holiday cheer, particularly during the festive season. The association of peppermint with Christmas is deeply rooted in its historical use as a digestive aid. During elaborate feasts, especially in medieval times, peppermint was employed to soothe the stomach after indulging in rich and hearty meals. This culinary tradition extended to the creation of peppermint-infused treats, marking the herb as a festive flavor that complements the celebratory spirit of Christmas. The iconic candy cane, with its red and white stripes and distinctive peppermint taste, embodies this cultural significance, symbolizing both the sweetness of the season and the purity of the Christmas story.

In North American traditions, peppermint has become ubiquitous during the winter holidays. The use of peppermint in holiday treats, beverages, and decorations is a testament to its role in creating a festive atmosphere.

Peppermint-flavored hot cocoa, candy canes adorning Christmas trees, and peppermint-infused desserts contribute to the sensory experience of the season. Additionally, peppermint's cool and invigorating essence aligns with the winter months, refreshingly contrasting with the chilly weather. The cultural significance of peppermint in North America is deeply ingrained in holiday customs, where its presence evokes a sense of warmth and nostalgia.

Moving eastward, peppermint takes on a unique significance in Asian traditions, particularly in the context of traditional Chinese medicine. In this cultural landscape, peppermint is valued not only for its culinary attributes but also for its therapeutic properties. The cooling nature of peppermint makes it a sought-after herb, especially during warmer seasons. Peppermint tea alleviates heat-related discomfort, providing a refreshing and revitalizing beverage. This dual role of peppermint as both a culinary delight and a remedy underscores its cultural importance, weaving seamlessly into the fabric of daily life and wellness practices.

In Middle Eastern traditions, peppermint finds its place in culinary and medicinal realms. Peppermint tea, known as "nana" or "nane," holds cultural significance as a popular beverage. It is often served in social gatherings and is considered a symbol of hospitality. Beyond its role as a beverage, peppermint's aromatic qualities contribute to the sensory experience of Middle Eastern cuisine. The herb is used in desserts, savory dishes, and as a refreshing ingredient in salads. The cultural symbolism of peppermint in the Middle East extends beyond its flavor, encompassing notions of friendliness, health, and culinary excellence.

In the Indian subcontinent, peppermint has carved a niche in traditional Ayurvedic practices. Known as "pudina," peppermint is celebrated for its cooling properties and is often used to balance the doshas, particularly during the scorching summer months. Peppermint-infused beverages and chutneys are enjoyed for their flavor and refreshing sense of refreshment. The cultural significance of peppermint in this context lies in its holistic approach to well-being, where the herb becomes a part of daily rituals that promote both physical and mental health.

Throughout Latin American cultures, peppermint has found its way into both traditional remedies and festive culinary creations. Peppermint tea, often prepared with fresh leaves, is embraced for its digestive benefits and is a popular choice for alleviating discomfort after meals. In the realm of celebrations, peppermint is incorporated into desserts and beverages during festive occasions, adding a touch of coolness to the vibrancy of Latin American cuisine. The cultural significance of peppermint here is a harmonious fusion of its healing properties and its ability to elevate the sensory experience of festive gatherings. In

African cultures, peppermint's cultural significance is expressed in diverse ways. In some regions, peppermint is cultivated and used in traditional medicine for its aromatic and digestive properties. The herb is incorporated into teas and infusions consumed for their soothing effects. In other contexts, where peppermint may not be native, its introduction into culinary practices symbolizes globalization and cross-cultural exchange. As peppermint-infused dishes become part of local culinary landscapes, they carry a nuanced cultural significance that transcends geographical boundaries.

In summary, the cultural significance of peppermint in different traditions reflects its multifaceted nature as both a culinary delight and a symbol of well-being. Across continents, peppermint weaves itself into the fabric of daily life, enhancing the sensory experience of food and drink while embodying cultural values related to hospitality, celebration, and health. Whether it's sipping peppermint tea in a Middle Eastern gathering, enjoying a candy cane during Christmas festivities, or savoring peppermint-infused desserts in Latin American celebrations, the cultural tapestry of peppermint is a testament to its enduring appeal and adaptability in diverse cultural contexts.

CHAPTER II

Peppermint and Candy Canes - A Sweet Affair

History and Symbolism of Candy Canes

The history and symbolism of candy canes weave a sweet tale that transcends generations, enchanting holiday celebrations with iconic red and white stripes and distinctive peppermint flavor. The candy cane's origins can be traced back to 17th-century Europe, where confectioners in Germany are credited with creating the first versions of what would become this enduring symbol of the festive season. The initial designs were likely simple, straight sticks of white sugar candy, but the characteristic hook shape and dual-toned stripes emerged over time.

One popular legend attributes the creation of the candy cane to a choir director in Cologne, Germany, in the late 1600s. Facing the challenge of keeping children quiet during long Christmas Eve ceremonies, the choirmaster supposedly sought the help of a local candy maker. Together, they fashioned white sugar sticks into canes with a hook at the top, symbolizing the shepherd's crook, as a way to keep children entertained while reminding them of the Christmas story.

The symbolic aspects of the candy cane gained prominence in the 18th century, particularly about Christmas. The white color of the candy cane is said to represent purity, while the red stripes are often interpreted as symbols of the blood of Christ. The incorporation of these elements transformed the candy cane into a meaningful treat, carrying religious significance that resonated with the themes of the Christmas season.

As the candy cane tradition spread across Europe, it found its way into various Christmas customs and celebrations. In the 19th century, the widespread use of Christmas trees became popular, and candy canes began to adorn these evergreen symbols of the holiday season. The candy cane's distinctive shape, reminiscent of a shepherd's crook or a "J" for Jesus, added to its symbolic significance as a Christmas confection.

The introduction of peppermint flavor to candy canes further enhanced their appeal. With its refreshing and invigorating taste, Peppermint became synonymous with the winter season, aligning perfectly with the festive atmosphere. The infusion of peppermint elevated the flavor profile of candy canes and contributed to their association with holiday merriment.

In the United States, the candy cane gained widespread popularity in the mid-20th century. Its presence on Christmas trees, in stockings, and as a popular treat during the holiday season became a cherished tradition. The iconic red and white stripes became more standardized, solidifying the candy cane's visual identity. Candy canes also became versatile decorations, blending into various holiday crafts and ornaments.

Today, the candy cane remains a beloved symbol of the Christmas season, cherished by people of all ages. Its enduring popularity is evident in the myriad ways it is incorporated into holiday traditions, from being used as a decorative element on Christmas trees to being enjoyed as a sweet treat. Candy cane-inspired products, from cookies to hot cocoa, further emphasize the candy cane's cultural resonance during the festive season.

Beyond its historical roots, the candy cane's symbolism has evolved to encompass a broader sense of joy, sweetness, and holiday spirit. The recognizable red and white stripes evoke a sense of nostalgia and tradition, making the candy cane a timeless emblem of the Christmas season. Its simple yet meaningful design continues to captivate the imagination and hearts of people worldwide, serving as a delightful reminder of the joyous traditions that define the holiday season.

Incorporating Candy Canes into Baking

Incorporating candy canes into baking is a festive culinary tradition that adds a touch of whimsy and a peppermint flavor to various sweet treats. The iconic red and white stripes of candy canes evoke the spirit of the holiday season, making them delightful decorations and versatile ingredients in the hands of bakers and home cooks. From classic cookies to decadent desserts, incorporating candy canes introduces a playful and visually appealing element to baked goods, creating treats that capture the essence of Christmas joy.

One of the most popular ways to utilize candy canes in baking is by incorporating them into cookie recipes. Peppermint-flavored cookies with pieces of crushed candy canes offer a delightful twist on traditional favorites. The candy cane bits not only infuse the cookies with a burst of minty freshness but also add a lovely crunch that elevates the texture of the baked goods. Peppermint chocolate chip cookies, whose rich chocolate is complemented by the excellent notes of crushed candy canes, have become a beloved holiday classic.

Candy canes also make a stunning addition to brownies and bars. Peppermint bark brownies offer a decadent and visually appealing treat, featuring layers of fudgy chocolate and a peppermint-infused white chocolate topping adorned with crushed candy canes. The combination of rich chocolate and the excellent, crisp texture of candy cane pieces creates a harmonious contrast that tantalizes the taste buds. These festive brownies have become a staple at holiday gatherings, capturing the essence of indulgence and merriment.

For those who enjoy the artistry of cake decorating, candy canes provide an excellent opportunity to showcase creativity. Peppermint swirl cupcakes, adorned with a candy cane or two, look charming and deliver a delightful fusion of flavors. The candy cane is a decorative topper and a built-in flavor enhancer, infusing the cupcake with a hint of peppermint that surprises and delights with each bite. Incorporating crushed candy canes into the frosting or batter of cakes adds a festive flair that transforms a simple dessert into a visually striking masterpiece.

Candy canes can also take center stage in the creation of show-stopping desserts. Peppermint cheesecake, with a crunchy candy cane crust and swirls of peppermint-infused filling, embodies the essence of holiday indulgence. Combining the creamy cheesecake and the crisp bits of candy cane creates a delightful contrast that appeals to both the palate and the eye. Peppermint bark ice cream, featuring ribbons of crushed candy canes, brings a refreshing and festive twist to a classic frozen treat.

In confections, candy canes are vital ingredients in creating delightful holiday treats. Peppermint bark, a layered confection of white and dark chocolate topped with crushed candy canes, has become synonymous with festive indulgence. The smooth, velvety chocolate pairs seamlessly with the crunchy, minty bits of candy cane, creating a visually stunning and delectably satisfying treat. Peppermint truffles, rolled in crushed candy canes, offer bite-sized delights that encapsulate the essence of holiday decadence.

Candy canes can also lend their enchanting flavor to beverages, transforming ordinary drinks into festive delights. Peppermint hot chocolate, garnished with a candy cane stirrer, brings a comforting warmth to chilly winter evenings. The slow melting of the candy cane infuses the hot chocolate with a subtle minty sweetness, creating a cozy and indulgent beverage that resonates with the season's flavors. Peppermint mochas and candy cane-infused cocktails further showcase the versatility of candy canes in beverages, offering delightful sips that capture the festive spirit.

Incorporating candy canes into baking extends beyond traditional recipes, inspiring inventive creations that push the boundaries of holiday treats. Candy cane macarons, featuring a peppermint-flavored filling and crushed candy canes as a decorative element, showcase the delicate artistry of French pastry combined with the season's festive spirit. Candy cane whoopie pies, with peppermint-infused frosting sandwiched between soft cake-like cookies, offer a handheld indulgence that is visually appealing and deliciously satisfying.

For those with dietary preferences or restrictions, candy canes can be incorporated into gluten-free, vegan, or allergen-friendly recipes, ensuring everyone can partake in the joy of holiday baking. Gluten-free candy cane brownies and vegan peppermint chocolate chip cookies are just a few examples of how the iconic flavors of candy canes can be adapted to accommodate various dietary needs, allowing everyone to enjoy the festive delights of holiday baking.

In conclusion, incorporating candy canes into baking is a delightful and creative endeavor that adds a festive touch to a wide array of sweet treats. From cookies and brownies to cakes and confections, the iconic red and white stripes and the refreshing peppermint flavor of candy canes elevate holiday baking to new heights.

Whether used as a decorative element, a flavor enhancer, or a key ingredient, candy canes bring a sense of joy and merriment to the kitchen, creating treats that capture the essence of the holiday season and delight both bakers and those fortunate enough to indulge in these delectable creations.

Candy Cane Decorations and Themes

Candy cane decorations and themes embody the festive spirit of the holiday season, transforming spaces into whimsical and joyful settings that captivate the imagination. The iconic red and white stripes of candy canes evoke a sense of nostalgia and merriment, making them a cherished element in holiday decor. From traditional ornaments on Christmas trees to elaborate themed displays, candy canes have become synonymous with the visual language of Christmas, infusing spaces with warmth, sweetness, and a touch of enchantment.

One of the most classic uses of candy cane decorations is adorning Christmas trees with these iconic treats. The candy canes' vibrant red and white hues add a lively and festive dimension to the evergreen backdrop. Whether hung individually as ornaments or intertwined with garlands, candy canes become integral elements that evoke the charm of Christmases past. The act of unwrapping a candy cane and savoring its peppermint goodness is a treat for the taste buds and a sensory experience that enhances the joy of decorating the tree. Candy cane-themed wreaths are another popular way to infuse holiday spaces with festive cheer. These wreaths, often crafted with candy canes and complementary ornaments, create a welcoming and visually striking entrance to homes. Whether displayed on doors, windows, or walls, candy cane wreaths encapsulate the season's essence, inviting guests into a space adorned with the timeless symbols of Christmas joy.

In table decor, candy cane centerpieces are eye-catching focal points for holiday gatherings. Vases filled with candy canes, interspersed with seasonal greenery or candles, create a delightful tableau that enhances the festive atmosphere. Candy cane place card holders and napkin rings extend the theme to individual settings, adding a touch of whimsy to holiday meals and celebrations. Combining the candy canes' vibrant colors and peppermint aroma transforms dining spaces into enchanting realms of seasonal delight.

For those with a penchant for crafting, candy cane-themed DIY projects offer an opportunity to infuse personal creativity into holiday decor. Handmade candy cane garlands, wreaths, and ornaments allow individuals to tailor their decor to specific color schemes or themes. Creating these decorations becomes a festive tradition, fostering a sense of joy and accomplishment as homemade candy cane decor adorns homes with a unique and personalized touch.

Candy cane archways and pathways create magical transitions between spaces, transforming hallways and entryways into whimsical realms of holiday enchantment. Arching strings of oversized candy canes or creating pathways lined with these festive symbols adds a playful and immersive element to home decor. The visual impact of walking through a candy cane arch is reminiscent of entering a sugary wonderland, elevating the experience of moving through decorated spaces.

In commercial and public spaces, candy cane decorations take on grand proportions, contributing to the festive ambiance of streets, shopping centers, and public events. Giant candy cane sculptures, illuminated with festive lights, become iconic landmarks that define the holiday season. The scale and creativity of these decorations extend beyond individual homes, creating a shared experience of joy and wonder for entire communities.

Candy cane themes extend beyond traditional red and white color schemes, offering versatility in holiday decor. Pastel candy cane themes featuring soft pink, blue, and green hues bring a contemporary and whimsical twist to classic decor. Incorporating metallic accents, such as gold or silver, elevates the elegance of candy cane-themed decorations, making them suitable for sophisticated holiday settings. Candy cane-inspired decor is not limited to indoor spaces; it can extend to outdoor landscapes, where oversized candy canes and themed lighting create a festive and inviting atmosphere.

In addition to decorations, candy cane themes inspire a variety of holiday celebrations and activities. Candy cane scavenger hunts, where participants search for hidden candy canes, add an element of excitement to festive gatherings. Candy cane-themed parties, with striped decorations, peppermint-flavored treats, and themed activities, create memorable experiences for children and adults. Incorporating candy cane themes into holiday festivities extends the joy of these iconic symbols beyond visual aesthetics, infusing the season's spirit into various aspects of celebrations.

Candy cane decorations and themes have also found a place in holiday events and displays. Festivals of lights often feature elaborate installations of oversized candy canes, creating dazzling spectacles that draw crowds and contribute to the overall magic of the season. Candy cane-themed Christmas markets, with stalls adorned in red and white stripes, offer a delightful shopping experience that combines the joy of gift-buying with the festive ambiance of the holidays.

In conclusion, candy cane decorations and themes have become integral elements of holiday decor, infusing spaces with the timeless symbols of Christmas joy and sweetness. From classic ornaments on Christmas trees to elaborate displays in public spaces, candy canes evoke a sense of nostalgia and merriment that resonates with people of all ages. The versatility of candy cane themes allows for creative expressions in various color schemes and settings, making them adaptable to different decor styles. Whether enjoyed as traditional ornaments, integrated into DIY projects, or incorporated into themed celebrations, candy canes continue to enchant and captivate, adding a touch of whimsy to the visual tapestry of the holiday season.

CHAPTER III

Essential Peppermint Ingredients and Tools

Exploring Varieties of Peppermint

Exploring peppermint varieties unveils this versatile herb's rich and aromatic world, renowned for its distinctive flavor, refreshing scent, and myriad applications across culinary, medicinal, and aromatic domains. Mentha × piperita, commonly known as peppermint, is a hybrid mint that stands out among its botanical counterparts for its robust flavor profile, characterized by a refreshing combination of cool menthol and sweet undertones. The exploration of peppermint varieties encompasses diverse cultivars and how this herb has adapted to different climates, soil conditions, and cultivation methods, giving rise to nuanced variations that cater to various preferences and uses.

One of the most well-known peppermint varieties is the traditional peppermint, recognized for its iconic combination of bold menthol notes and underlying sweetness. This classic cultivar is widely used in culinary applications, finding its way into teas, candies, desserts, and savory dishes. The balance of cooling menthol and a hint of sweetness makes traditional peppermint a go-to choice for those seeking the quintessential mint experience. Its adaptability to different growing conditions has made it a staple in gardens and commercial cultivation, ensuring a steady supply of this beloved herb for diverse purposes.

Although distinct from traditional peppermint, Spearmint is often considered part of the broader peppermint family due to its shared genus, Mentha. Spearmint (Mentha spicata) boasts a milder and sweeter flavor than peppermint, making it a popular choice for culinary applications. Its bright green leaves and subtle menthol notes contribute a refreshing and less intense minty character to beverages, salads, and desserts. Spearmint's versatility extends beyond the kitchen; its essential oil is widely used for aromatherapy and personal care products, offering a fragrant and uplifting experience.

In peppermint cultivars, variations in menthol content, flavor intensity, and aroma have given rise to unique profiles that cater to specific preferences. For example, with its infusion of chocolate undertones, chocolate mint adds a delightful twist to the traditional peppermint flavor. This cultivar is a favorite in desserts, where its nuanced profile complements the richness of chocolate-based treats. On the other hand, Lemon mint introduces citrusy notes to the peppermint experience, creating a zesty and aromatic herb that elevates sweet and savory dishes. The cultivation of peppermint varieties extends beyond individual characteristics to the conditions under which they are grown. Organic peppermint, cultivated without synthetic pesticides or fertilizers, has gained popularity among those seeking a natural and environmentally conscious option. Organic cultivation emphasizes sustainable practices, allowing the herb to flourish in a nutrient-rich environment. The resulting organic peppermint is often prized for its purity of flavor and aromatic qualities, appealing to those who prefer clean and eco-friendly products.

Regional variations in peppermint cultivation also contribute to the diversity of available varieties. Peppermint grown in different climates and soil conditions can exhibit subtle differences in flavor and aroma. For example, peppermint cultivated in the Pacific Northwest of the United States is known for its high menthol content and robust flavor. This regional specificity is attributed to the combination of cool temperatures and fertile soil, creating an ideal environment for peppermint cultivation. In contrast, peppermint grown in regions with warmer climates may showcase a slightly milder profile, influenced by the interplay of temperature, sunlight, and soil composition.

Beyond the culinary realm, the medicinal uses of peppermint have further fueled exploration into its varieties. Peppermint has a long history of therapeutic applications, and different varieties may offer nuanced benefits. For instance, the high menthol content in traditional peppermint is associated with soothing digestive discomfort and alleviating symptoms of irritable bowel syndrome (IBS). Peppermint essential oil derived from specific varieties is also valued for its antimicrobial properties, making it a popular ingredient in natural remedies for respiratory issues and headaches.

The world of peppermint extends to beverages, where its varieties play a crucial role in crafting diverse teas and infusions. Peppermint tea, made from the leaves of the traditional peppermint plant, is celebrated for its ability to soothe digestion, alleviate stress, and provide a caffeine-free option for tea enthusiasts. Peppermint tea's refreshing and invigorating qualities have led to the exploration of different varieties, each contributing subtle nuances to the overall tea experience. With its milder flavor, Spearmint has found a place in herbal blends, offering a gentler alternative for those seeking a minty infusion without the intensity of traditional peppermint. Peppermint's aromatic appeal extends to essential oils, where distillation methods capture its concentrated essence. Peppermint essential oil, derived from various peppermint varieties, is prized for its versatility. Its refreshing scent promotes alertness and focus, making it a popular choice for aromatherapy. Whether diffused in the air, added to personal care products, or used in massage oils, peppermint essential oil offers a sensory experience that transcends its culinary and medicinal applications.

The exploration of peppermint varieties is not only a journey into the nuances of flavor and aroma but also a testament to the adaptability and resilience of this herb. Peppermint's ability to thrive in diverse conditions, coupled with the artistry of cultivation and selective breeding, has given rise to a spectrum of varieties that cater to various preferences and uses. From the classic allure of traditional peppermint to the playful notes of chocolate mint and the citrusy brightness of lemon mint, the world of peppermint invites enthusiasts to savor the richness of this herb in its many forms. Whether enjoyed in a comforting cup of tea, incorporated into culinary creations, or experienced through the refreshing notes of essential oil, the peppermint varieties offer a delightful exploration of nature's aromatic treasures.

Key Ingredients for Peppermint-Infused Cookies

Creating the perfect peppermint-infused cookies is an art form that combines the rich, cooling essence of peppermint with the delightful sweetness of baked goods. The key ingredients for these cookies form a symphony of flavors, textures, and aromas that elevate the cookie-baking experience to a festive celebration. In the heart of this culinary adventure lies the star ingredient – peppermint – which imparts its signature coolness and invigorating notes to every bite.

Flour is the foundation for any cookie recipe, providing structure and texture. All-purpose flour is a versatile choice for peppermint-infused cookies, offering the right balance of protein and starch for a tender yet chewy consistency. Some bakers may opt for a combination of all-purpose and cake flour to achieve a softer texture, especially in recipes where a delicate crumb is desired. The choice of flour sets the stage for the overall mouthfeel of the cookies, ensuring a delightful balance between lightness and substance.

The buttery richness of unsalted butter is crucial in imparting a luxurious flavor and texture to peppermint cookies. Its fat content contributes to the cookies' tenderness, while its subtle nuttiness enhances the overall depth of flavor. Creaming the butter with sugar, a standard step in cookie recipes, incorporates air into the mixture, resulting in a light and fluffy texture. This process, crucial for achieving the perfect cookie consistency, ensures that the peppermint flavor is evenly distributed throughout the dough.

Sugar, both granulated and confectioners', brings sweetness to the cookies while contributing to their structure. Granulated sugar provides sweetness and helps create a slightly crispy exterior, while confectioners' sugar, with its fine texture, adds a delicate tenderness to the cookies. The balance between these sugars is crucial in achieving the desired sweetness level without overwhelming the refreshing notes of peppermint. Brown sugar can also be incorporated for a chewier texture, bringing a subtle molasses undertone that complements the overall flavor profile.

Eggs act as binders in the cookie dough, holding the ingredients together and contributing to the structure and texture of the final product. They also add moisture, aiding in developing a soft and chewy interior. In peppermint-infused cookies, the eggs create a cohesive dough that seamlessly incorporates the peppermint flavor. Some recipes may call for additional egg yolks to intensify the richness and chewiness of the cookies.

Peppermint extract is the soul of peppermint-infused cookies, infusing the dough with its distinctive cool and minty essence. Care should be taken to use pure peppermint extract to ensure an authentic and robust flavor. The amount of peppermint extract can be adjusted to personal preference, ranging from a subtle hint to an intense burst of mint. In addition to extract, finely crushed peppermint candies or candy canes can be added to the dough for a textural contrast and bursts of peppermint sweetness.

Vanilla extract enhances the overall flavor profile of the cookies, adding warmth and depth. Its subtle sweetness complements the peppermint, creating a harmonious blend of flavors. Pure vanilla extract is preferred for its rich and authentic taste, elevating the overall quality of the cookies. In some recipes, vanilla bean seeds or paste may impart a visual touch of vanilla specks and a more intense flavor.

Baking powder and baking soda are leavening agents contributing to the cookies' rise and texture. Baking powder provides a quick lift while baking soda helps with browning and contributes to the cookies' tenderness. The right balance of these leavening agents ensures a perfect rise without compromising the structural integrity of the cookies. The choice between the two or a combination thereof depends on the desired characteristics of the cookies, whether a cakey or chewy texture is preferred. Salt

is a crucial component that enhances the overall flavor profile of the cookies. It acts as a flavor amplifier, heightening the sugar's sweetness and the butter's richness. A pinch of salt helps balance the sweetness in peppermint-infused cookies, ensuring that the minty notes shine through without being overshadowed. Sea salt or kosher salt is often preferred for its clean and nuanced flavor.

Chocolate can be a delightful addition to peppermint-infused cookies, whether in the form of chips, chunks, or finely chopped bars. The combination of chocolate and peppermint creates a classic pairing reminiscent of mint chocolate treats. Dark chocolate, with its intense cocoa flavor, complements the coolness of peppermint, while milk chocolate adds a touch of creaminess. White chocolate, with its sweet and vanilla notes, provides a visually appealing contrast and a milder sweetness.

Nuts, such as chopped walnuts or pecans, contribute a delightful crunch and nutty flavor to peppermint cookies. Adding nuts enhances the texture and introduces a layer of complexity to the flavor profile. Toasting the nuts before incorporating them into the dough intensifies their nuttiness, creating a more robust and aromatic cookie experience. Nuts are often chosen based on personal preference, and their inclusion can be adapted to suit various dietary considerations.

The choice of flour, sugar, butter, eggs, extracts, leavening agents, and additional flavorings lays the groundwork for crafting the perfect peppermint-infused cookies. However, the success of the baking process also relies on techniques such as proper mixing, chilling the dough, and precision in measuring ingredients. Understanding the role of each ingredient and following a well-crafted recipe ensures that the cookies achieve the desired balance of flavors, textures, and aromas.

The process of baking peppermint-infused cookies extends beyond the technical aspects to become a sensory experience that evokes the joy and warmth of the holiday season. As the dough comes together, the kitchen is filled with the enticing aroma of peppermint, creating an atmosphere of anticipation. Shaping the dough into classic rounds, festive shapes, or elegant crescents adds a personal touch to the cookies and transforms them into edible works of art.

Baking the cookies in a preheated oven allows the ingredients to meld, creating a symphony of flavors as the peppermint mingles with the sweetness of sugar, the richness of butter, and the depth of vanilla. The cookies take on a golden hue, and the kitchen is once again filled with the irresistible scent of freshly baked treats. The careful monitoring of baking time ensures that the cookies balance between a lightly golden exterior and a soft, chewy interior.

Once out of the oven, the cookies cool on racks, their aromas inviting eager taste testers to experience the culmination of the baking journey. The final touch may include a drizzle of chocolate, a dusting of powdered sugar, or a sprinkle of crushed peppermint candies, adding visual appeal and additional layers of flavor. The cookies are now ready to be shared, gifted, or enjoyed with a cup of peppermint tea or hot cocoa, creating moments of sweetness and connection during the holiday season.

In conclusion, the key ingredients for peppermint-infused cookies form a palette of flavors and textures that come together to create a festive and delectable treat. The careful selection and balance of flour, sugar, butter, eggs, extracts, leavening agents, and additional flavorings contribute to the overall success of the baking process. Beyond the technical aspects, baking peppermint cookies is a sensory and joyful experience that captures the essence of the holiday season. As these cookies emerge from the oven, they carry with them the kitchen's warmth, peppermint's aroma, and the promise of delightful moments shared with loved ones.

Must-Have Tools for Peppermint Perfection

Achieving peppermint perfection in your culinary creations requires the right ingredients and a selection of must-have tools that streamline the baking process and ensure precision in every step. From mixing to shaping and baking, the journey to peppermint perfection involves a careful dance between artistry and technique. These essential tools simplify the process and contribute to the overall success and enjoyment of crafting peppermint-infused treats.

The foundation of any successful baking endeavor lies in accurate measurements, and a set of measuring cups and spoons is a fundamental tool in the kitchen. Precision in measuring flour, sugar, and other dry ingredients is crucial to achieving the right balance of flavors and textures in peppermint-infused cookies. Additionally, measuring spoons is indispensable when incorporating extracts and spices, ensuring that the peppermint essence is neither overpowering nor subtle.

A stand or a reliable hand mixer is a game-changer in cookie baking. Creaming butter and sugar to the ideal light and fluffy consistency is critical in creating the perfect cookie texture. A mixer expedites this process, saving time and effort while ensuring uniformity in the dough. The ability to control the speed of the mixer allows for precise blending, contributing to the overall quality of the cookies.

In pursuing peppermint perfection, incorporating peppermint extract into the cookie dough requires finesse. A quality peppermint extract is essential, and a small measuring spoon ensures accuracy in adding just the right amount. The goal is to infuse the dough with the refreshing essence of peppermint without overwhelming the other flavors. The precision offered by a measuring spoon plays a crucial role in achieving this delicate balance.

Mixing bowls, both stainless steel and glass, are versatile and indispensable tools in the cookie-making process. Whether blending dry ingredients, creaming butter and sugar, or folding in chocolate chips and nuts, having an array of mixing bowls in various sizes accommodates different stages of the recipe. The ease of cleaning and durability of stainless steel, along with the transparency of glass, allow bakers to choose based on their preferences.

A silicone spatula becomes a trusty companion in the kitchen, facilitating the smooth incorporation of ingredients and ensuring no remnants of cookie dough are left behind. Its flexibility allows for thorough scraping of bowls and mixers, minimizing waste and ensuring that every bit of the peppermint-infused dough contributes to the final product. Additionally, a spatula proves invaluable when folding in delicate additions like chocolate chips or crushed peppermint candies.

Precision in shaping and portioning the cookie dough is where a cookie scoop comes into play. This tool ensures uniformity in size, resulting in evenly baked cookies. Whether creating classic rounds or experimenting with festive shapes, a cookie scoop streamlines the process, saving time and effort while contributing to the visual appeal of the final product. The ease of use and consistent results make a cookie scoop essential for achieving peppermint perfection.

Rolling traditional and adjustable pins are indispensable for recipes that involve rolling out cookie dough. For peppermint-infused cookies that require a uniform thickness, a rolling pin ensures even baking and a consistent texture. Adjustable rolling pins with thickness guides offer precision, allowing bakers to achieve the desired thickness for various types of cookies, from cutouts to filled varieties.

Baking sheets or cookie sheets with non-stick surfaces are essential for perfect baking. Their flat and even surfaces ensure uniform heat distribution, preventing cookies from sticking and promoting even browning. Parchment paper or silicone baking mats are valuable additions, providing a non-stick surface that simplifies cleanup and allows for easy removal of cookies from the baking sheet.

Oven thermometers play a crucial role in ensuring accurate baking temperatures. Ovens can vary in temperature accuracy, and an oven thermometer assures the cookies are balking at the intended temperature. Achieving the right balance between a golden exterior and a tender interior relies on precise temperature control, making an oven thermometer an invaluable tool in pursuing peppermint perfection.

Cooling racks allow cookies to cool evenly and quickly after baking. Elevating the cookies on a cooling rack prevents condensation when placing them directly on a surface. Proper cooling ensures that the peppermint-infused cookies maintain their intended texture, preventing sogginess and allowing for easy handling and decorating.

Cookie cutters add a festive touch to peppermint-infused cookies, especially during the holiday season. Whether creating classic shapes like rounds and stars or opting for whimsical holiday motifs, cookie cutters allow creative expression. The variety of shapes and sizes enables bakers to tailor their creations to different occasions, enhancing the visual appeal of the cookies.

Piping bags and tips open up possibilities for decorating peppermint treats. From drizzling chocolate over cookies to creating intricate designs with icing, piping bags provide precision and control. Various tips allow for decorative elements, from delicate swirls to complex patterns. Decorating with a piping bag will enable bakers to add a personal and artistic touch to their peppermint creations.

Quality bakeware, including sturdy baking pans and sheets, contributes to the overall success of the baking process. Invest in pans that distribute heat evenly and withstand repeated use. Non-stick surfaces promote easy release, ensuring peppermint-infused cookies maintain their intended shapes and textures. Durable bakeware is an investment that pays off in consistent and reliable results.

A kitchen timer is a simple yet invaluable tool in pursuing peppermint perfection. With precise baking times crucial for achieving the desired texture, a reliable timer ensures that cookies are fresh and dry. The audible alert serves as a reminder, allowing bakers to focus on other tasks without the risk of forgetting about the cookies in the oven.

Pastry brushes, particularly those with silicone bristles, are handy tools for applying egg washes or melted chocolate to peppermint cookies. This adds a glossy finish to the cookies, enhances their visual appeal, and can even be an adhesive for decorative elements like crushed peppermint candies. Pastry brushes provide a delicate touch, ensuring even application without compromising the cookies' structure.

Microplane graters or zesters offer a convenient way to incorporate citrus zest into peppermint-infused cookies. The fine texture achieved with a microplane ensures an even distribution of zest throughout the dough, adding a burst of citrusy brightness that complements the coolness of peppermint. This tool provides precision and control, allowing bakers to tailor the level of citrus flavor to their preferences.

Decorative stencils and brushes are optional but delightful tools for those who wish to add artistic elements to their peppermint cookies. Stencils create intricate patterns, while small brushes allow for carefully applying edible powders or glitters. These tools open up opportunities for creative expression, turning cookies into edible canvases that reflect the baker's artistic flair.

In conclusion, the journey to peppermint perfection in baking is paved with many must-have tools that enhance the process and contribute to the overall success of creating delectable treats. From precise measurements with measuring cups and spoons to decorating with piping bags and tips, each tool uniquely brings the vision of peppermint-infused cookies to life. As bakers embark on this flavorful adventure, carefully selecting and utilizing these tools ensure a seamless and enjoyable experience, resulting in cookies that embody the essence of peppermint perfection.

CHAPTER IV

Classic Peppermint Cookie Recipes

Peppermint Chocolate Chip Cookies

Peppermint and chocolate, when combined, create a harmonious symphony of flavors that captivates the senses and evokes the festive spirit of the holiday season. Among the myriad holiday treats, Peppermint Chocolate Chip Cookies stand out as a delightful fusion of cool, refreshing peppermint and chocolate's rich, indulgent sweetness. This beloved cookie variation transforms the familiar chocolate chip cookie into a seasonal delight, offering a burst of minty freshness that complements the comforting familiarity of chocolate.

At the heart of Peppermint Chocolate Chip Cookies is the marriage of two iconic ingredients—peppermint and chocolate chips. The journey to crafting these delectable cookies begins with carefully selecting quality peppermint extract, ensuring an authentic and robust mint flavor that infuses the entire cookie. The essence of peppermint is a key player, providing a relaxed and refreshing note that elevates the cookie-eating experience to a festive celebration.

The chocolate chips, nestled within the cookie dough, add complexity to the flavor profile. Choosing between dark chocolate, milk chocolate, or a combination of both allows for a tailored approach to sweetness and cocoa intensity. The melting chocolate chips contribute gooey pockets of richness, contrasting peppermint's coolness and adding a satisfying texture to every bite.

Creating Peppermint Chocolate Chip Cookies involves meticulously blending wet and dry ingredients, allowing the flavors to meld seamlessly. The familiar steps of creaming butter and sugar take a holiday twist as peppermint extract is incorporated, infusing the dough with its refreshing essence. Adding eggs and vanilla further enriches the dough, creating a foundation for the peppermint and chocolate to shine.

The art of baking Peppermint Chocolate Chip Cookies lies in achieving the perfect balance between peppermint's intensity and chocolate's sweetness. Careful measurement of peppermint extract ensures that the cookies deliver a burst of minty freshness without overpowering the overall flavor. The amount of chocolate chips generously scattered throughout the dough can be adjusted to personal preference, allowing for a harmonious interplay of flavors.

The kitchen is filled with the irresistible aroma of peppermint and chocolate melding together as the cookie dough takes shape. The anticipation builds as the cookies turn in the oven, transforming into golden discs of holiday bliss. The scent wafting through the kitchen is a testament to the magic that happens when peppermint and chocolate unite, creating a sensory experience that transcends the act of baking.

Upon emerging from the oven, Peppermint Chocolate Chip Cookies display a visual allure that mirrors the festive season. The golden edges and melty chocolate chips beckon, inviting eager taste testers to savor the culmination of the baking journey. The first bite reveals a tender interior, a subtle crunch on the edges, and a burst of peppermint freshness that dances on the taste buds. The combination of warm, gooey chocolate and cool peppermint creates a sensory contrast that defines the uniqueness of these holiday cookies.

The versatility of Peppermint Chocolate Chip Cookies extends beyond their delicious simplicity. These cookies can take on various forms, from classic rounds to festive shapes that capture the season's essence. Whether adorned with a dusting of powdered sugar, a drizzle of chocolate, or a sprinkle of crushed candy canes, the cookies become edible works of art, adding a visual delight to holiday gatherings.

The appeal of Peppermint Chocolate Chip Cookies lies not only in their delightful taste but also in their ability to evoke cherished memories of holiday traditions. Baking these cookies becomes a festive ritual, a shared experience that brings loved ones together in the kitchen's warmth. The aroma of baking cookies becomes a fragrant reminder of holidays past and a promise of joy for the present.

For those with a penchant for creativity, Peppermint Chocolate Chip Cookies offer a canvas for festive decorating. Adding peppermint-flavored icing, swirls of chocolate ganache, or a sprinkle of edible glitter transforms each cookie into a miniature work of art. The decorating process becomes an opportunity for self-expression, allowing bakers to tailor their creations to the theme of their holiday celebrations.

The versatility of Peppermint Chocolate Chip Cookies extends beyond home kitchens to become delightful additions to holiday gatherings, cookie exchanges, and festive dessert tables. Packaged in festive boxes or tied with ribbon, these cookies make thoughtful gifts that embody the season's spirit. Their visual appeal, combined with the irresistible blend of peppermint and chocolate, ensures they stand out among the holiday treats.

For those who relish the opportunity to experiment, Peppermint Chocolate Chip Cookies can be customized to cater to different dietary preferences. Whether using gluten-free flour, dairy-free chocolate chips, or incorporating alternative sweeteners, the basic recipe serves as a versatile foundation for creating inclusive treats that a diverse range of cookie enthusiasts can enjoy.

In conclusion, Peppermint Chocolate Chip Cookies are more than a seasonal confection; they celebrate the holiday spirit captured in a single bite. The synergy of peppermint and chocolate creates a sensory experience that transcends the act of baking, inviting individuals to savor the joy of the season. Whether enjoyed with a cup of hot cocoa, shared with loved ones, or gifted as tokens of festive cheer, these cookies embody the magic of the holidays and the simple pleasures of the union of classic flavors. Peppermint Chocolate Chip Cookies are not just cookies; they are a festive tradition, a flavorful journey, and a sweet reminder of the warmth accompanying the season's celebrations.

Candy Cane Sugar Cookies

Candy canes, with their iconic red-and-white stripes, are synonymous with the festive spirit of the holiday season. Infusing the essence of these beloved confections into sugar cookies creates a delightful marriage of tradition and whimsy. Candy Cane Sugar Cookies emerge as a seasonal treat that pays homage to the classic sugar cookie and adds a visually striking and flavor-packed element to the holiday table.

The journey to crafting Candy Cane Sugar Cookies begins with the familiar ritual of measuring flour, sugar, and butter. However, the whimsical twist comes with adding finely crushed candy canes to the dough. These sugary morsels impart a peppermint flavor and create a festive visual element, sprinkling the dough with hints of red. The choice of quality candy canes ensures an authentic and robust minty essence that harmonizes with the sweetness of the sugar cookies.

Creating Candy Cane Sugar Cookies mirrors traditional sugar cookies, involving the creaming of butter and sugar to achieve the ideal light and fluffy consistency. Adding eggs and vanilla enriches the dough, providing a foundation for the peppermint infusion. As the finely crushed candy canes are incorporated, the kitchen is filled with the irresistible aroma of mint, creating an atmosphere that captures the essence of holiday baking. Rolling out the Candy Cane Sugar Cookie dough introduces another layer of creativity. Incorporating candy cane-inspired swirls, combined with plain and peppermint-infused dough, adds a whimsical visual element to the cookies. The red-and-white swirls pay homage to the candy canes' iconic design, creating a striking contrast that transforms each cookie into a miniature edible art. The magic of Candy Cane Sugar Cookies truly comes to life in the oven. As the cookies bake, the candy cane-infused dough spreads, creating swirls of red that mimic the patterns found on traditional candy canes. The transformation is visual and olfactory, as the warm scent of peppermint fills the kitchen, heightening the anticipation of the delicious treats about to emerge.

Upon emerging from the oven, Candy Cane Sugar Cookies display a visual allure that captures the notion of the season. The golden edges provide a subtle crunch, while the interior remains tender and buttery. Now set in the cookie's structure, the candy cane swirls create a festive appearance that invites both admiration and anticipation. Their peppermint-infused charm makes these cookies a positive addition to holiday gatherings and cookie exchanges.

The experience of biting into a Candy Cane Sugar Cookie is a sensory delight. The initial crunch gives way to a buttery tenderness, and the burst of peppermint flavor adds a refreshing coolness that lingers on the palate. The interplay of sweetness and minty freshness creates a harmonious balance, making these cookies stand out among holiday treats. The visual appeal and the delectable combination of flavors ensure that Candy Cane Sugar Cookies become a sought-after indulgence during the festive season.

The versatility of Candy Cane Sugar Cookies extends beyond their delightful taste to their potential for creative presentation. These cookies can be shaped into classic rounds, festive stars, or whimsical candy cane shapes, allowing for artistic expression in the baking process. Adding a dusting of powdered sugar or a drizzle of white chocolate enhances their visual appeal, turning them into edible ornaments and contributing to the holiday ambiance.

Decorating Candy Cane Sugar Cookies provides an opportunity for personalization and creativity. Royal icing, tinted in festive colors, can add intricate designs or outline the candy cane swirls, creating a polished and professional look. Edible glitter or sprinkles can be strategically applied to enhance the holiday theme further, turning each cookie into a miniature canvas for artistic expression.

The festive charm of Candy Cane Sugar Cookies extends to their role in holiday celebrations. Whether served at a family gathering, in a dessert spread or given as thoughtful gifts, these cookies evoke the season's spirit. Packaged in festive boxes or adorned with ribbons, Candy Cane Sugar Cookies become a delicious treat and a positive gesture that embodies the joy of giving during the holidays.

For those passionate about hosting holiday events, Candy Cane Sugar Cookies can become a dessert table centerpiece or a delightful cookie exchange addition. Their whimsical appearance adds a touch of magic to the spread, and the combination of flavors ensures that they stand out among the seasonal treats. These cookies become a dessert and conversation piece, sparking joy and admiration among guests.

The customization of Candy Cane Sugar Cookies also extends to accommodating dietary preferences. These cookies can be adapted to suit various dietary needs with gluten-free flour, dairy-free butter, and alternative sweeteners. The joy of indulging in a festive treat becomes inclusive, allowing individuals with different nutritional considerations to partake in the holiday sweetness.

In conclusion, Candy Cane Sugar Cookies are more than a seasonal indulgence; they celebrate the holiday spirit captured in every swirl and bite. The fusion of peppermint with the classic sugar cookie creates a delightful treat that embodies tradition and whimsy. Whether enjoyed with a cup of hot cocoa, shared with loved ones, or gifted as tokens of festive cheer, these cookies encapsulate the magic of the holidays in a delectable form. Candy Cane Sugar Cookies are not just cookies; they are a festive tradition, a visual delight, and a sweet reminder of the joy accompanying the season's celebrations.

Peppermint Shortbread Delights

Peppermint Shortbread stands as a testament to the exquisite marriage of simplicity and sophistication in the realm of holiday baking. With its rich buttery texture and a burst of cool mintiness, this classic cookie elevates the holiday dessert experience to a realm of sheer delight. Peppermint Shortbread Delights encapsulate the season's essence, offering a perfect balance of indulgence and festive freshness.

At the heart of Peppermint Shortbread is the artistry of simplicity. The foundational ingredients—butter, sugar, flour, and a hint of peppermint extract—are transformed into a delicate dough that captures the essence of the holiday spirit. The process begins with the meticulous creaming of butter and sugar, a ritual that imparts a luscious texture and a buttery richness to the shortbread. Adding flour creates a tender crumb that melts in the mouth, establishing the foundation for the subtle peppermint infusion.

Peppermint extract, carefully measured and added to the dough, introduces a refreshing twist that sets this shortbread apart. The choice of quality peppermint extract is paramount, ensuring an authentic and refreshing mint flavor that dances on the taste buds. The subtle nature of peppermint in shortbread allows for a nuanced experience, where the minty freshness complements rather than overpowers the delicate buttery notes.

Shaping Peppermint Shortbread Delights involves a delicate process that highlights the elegance inherent in this classic treat. The dough can be fashioned into simple rounds, dainty fingers, or festive shapes that capture the holiday spirit. The use of cookie cutters allows for creative expression, turning the shortbread into edible ornaments that embody the lively charm of the season.

Baking Peppermint Shortbread is a transformative experience for both the kitchen and the senses. As the shortbread emerges from the oven, the golden edges and the buttery aroma create an anticipation of the delectable treat that awaits. The visual appeal of the shortbread, with its delicate crumb and a hint of peppermint, captures the essence of holiday elegance, making it a fitting addition to any festive gathering.

The first bite of Peppermint Shortbread Delights is an experience that transcends the ordinary. The initial crunch gives way to a delicate buttery crumb that lingers on the palate. The subtlety of peppermint unfolds gradually, creating a refreshing finish that complements the richness of the shortbread. The combination of textures and flavors results in a symphony of sophisticated and comforting taste.

The versatility of Peppermint Shortbread extends beyond its delectable taste to its potential for creative presentation. These cookies can be adorned with powdered sugar, a drizzle of white chocolate, or a sprinkle of crushed peppermint candies. The simplicity of shortbread becomes a canvas for artistic expression, allowing bakers to tailor the appearance of their creations to the theme of their holiday celebrations.

The festive charm of Peppermint Shortbread Delights is not confined to the realm of home kitchens; these cookies are poised to become stars of holiday dessert tables, cookie exchanges, and festive gift baskets. Packaged in elegant boxes or tied with festive ribbons, Peppermint Shortbread becomes a thoughtful and delightful gift embodying the season's spirit. The visual allure and exquisite taste ensure these shortbread delights leave a lasting impression on recipients.

Peppermint Shortbread provides an opportunity to experiment and personalize for those who revel in the joy of holiday baking. Adding finely chopped peppermint candies or chocolate chips to the dough introduces delightful surprises, creating a playful twist on the classic. Incorporating various shapes and sizes allows for a visually dynamic presentation, turning the shortbread into a centerpiece of festive dessert spreads.

Decorating Peppermint Shortbread can be a creative endeavor that adds a touch of flair to the classic treat. Royal icing in festive colors can create intricate designs or outline the edges, enhancing the visual appeal. Edible glitter or shimmering sugar transforms the shortbread into a dazzling display, reflecting the holiday spirit in every shimmer. Decorating becomes a joyful expression of individual style, turning each shortbread into a tiny edible art.

The charm of Peppermint Shortbread extends to its role as a versatile accompaniment to holiday beverages. Paired with a cup of hot cocoa, a festive latte, or a comforting tea, these shortbread delights to enhance the overall indulgence of the moment. The buttery richness complements the warmth of the drink, while the hint of peppermint provides a refreshing contrast, creating a delightful symphony for the taste buds.

The adaptability of Peppermint Shortbread allows for inclusive enjoyment, catering to various dietary preferences. With gluten-free flour and dairy-free butter alternatives, these shortbread delights can be crafted to accommodate individuals with specific nutritional needs. The joy of savoring a festive treat becomes accessible to a broader audience, ensuring everyone can enjoy the holiday sweetness.

In conclusion, Peppermint Shortbread Delights are more than a seasonal confection; they celebrate the holiday spirit captured in every delicate bite. The synergy of buttery elegance and minty freshness creates a sensory experience that transcends the act of baking, inviting individuals to savor the joy of the season. Whether enjoyed with a cup of tea, shared with loved ones, or presented as a thoughtful gift, these shortbread delights encapsulate the magic of the holidays in a form that is both timeless and delightful. Peppermint Shortbread is not just a cookie; it is a festive tradition, a refined indulgence, and a sweet reminder of the joy accompanying the season's celebrations.

CHAPTER V

Beyond Cookies - Peppermint Treats Extravaganza

Peppermint Bark Brownies

In the realm of holiday desserts, Peppermint Bark Brownies emerge as a decadent indulgence that seamlessly marries the richness of chocolate with the festive freshness of peppermint. This delightful fusion transforms the classic brownie into a seasonal sensation, creating a symphony of flavors and textures that captivate the taste buds. Peppermint Bark Brownies embody the essence of the holiday spirit and serve as a visually stunning centerpiece for festive gatherings.

At the heart of Peppermint Bark Brownies lies the art of balancing rich, fudgy brownie goodness with the excellent, refreshing essence of peppermint bark. The process begins with the meticulous preparation of the brownie batter, a harmonious blend of high-quality chocolate, butter, sugar, eggs, and flour. The careful selection of ingredients sets the stage for the luscious, chocolatey base that forms the canvas for infusing peppermint flavors.

Peppermint Bark Brownies' magic unfolds with the incorporation of peppermint extract into the brownie batter. This key ingredient introduces a refreshing twist, infusing the brownies with a subtle minty essence that elevates them beyond the ordinary. The choice of peppermint extract is crucial, as it determines the balance between the rich chocolate and the refreshing peppermint, ensuring a nuanced and delightful experience with each bite.

The creative layering process begins as the brownie batter is poured into the baking pan, creating a foundation for the following decadent layers. Introducing a velvety layer of white chocolate studded with finely crushed peppermint candies transforms the classic brownie into a festive masterpiece. The contrasting colors and textures add visual appeal and contribute to the overall sensory experience.

Baking Peppermint Bark Brownies is a compelling journey for the senses. As the brownies take shape in the oven, the kitchen is enveloped in the irresistible aroma of chocolate mingling with peppermint. The anticipation builds as the layers meld together, creating a symphony of scents that foreshadows the decadence about to be unveiled. The visual transformation adds to the excitement, from a glossy brownie layer to a swirled white chocolate-peppermint topping.

Upon emerging from the oven, Peppermint Bark Brownies reveal their visual allure. The glossy surface of the brownie layer, now adorned with swirls of white chocolate and flecks of peppermint candy, creates a festive mosaic that hints at the delectable layers within. The marriage of rich chocolate and cool peppermint is visually represented in every slice, making these brownies a stunning addition to holiday dessert displays.

The first bite of Peppermint Bark Brownies is an indulgent experience that surpasses expectations. The initial encounter with the fudgy brownie layer, dense and velvety, gives way to the creamy richness of the white chocolate-peppermint topping. The peppermint candy crunch adds a delightful textural contrast while the refreshing minty finish lingers on the palate. The combination of flavors creates a decadent symphony that elevates the brownie-eating experience to new heights.

The versatility of Peppermint Bark Brownies extends beyond their decadent taste to their role as a show-stopping dessert for holiday celebrations. The presentation of these brownies, adorned with festive swirls and a dusting of crushed peppermint, transforms them into a visual centerpiece that captures the season's spirit. Served on elegant platters or wrapped in festive packaging, Peppermint Bark Brownies become a dessert and a gift-worthy indulgence.

The allure of Peppermint Bark Brownies lies in their delicious simplicity and their potential for creative customization. Adding extra layers, such as a dark chocolate ganache or a peppermint-infused swirl, allows bakers to experiment with different textures and intensities of flavor. The decorative options, from drizzles of white chocolate to a sprinkle of edible glitter, provide an opportunity for artistic expression, turning each brownie into a unique creation.

The role of Peppermint Bark Brownies in holiday festivities extends to their potential as a thoughtful gift. Packaged in festive boxes, tied with ribbons, or placed in decorative tins, these brownies become tokens of festive cheer that are eagerly received. The visual appeal, combined with the luxurious taste, ensures they stand out among the array of holiday treats, making them a delightful gift for friends, family, and colleagues.

The adaptability of Peppermint Bark Brownies to different occasions makes them a versatile addition to holiday dessert tables. Whether served at a family gathering, in a dessert spread or brought to a festive potluck, these brownies become a conversation piece that elicits admiration and appreciation. Their decadence transforms ordinary moments into indulgent celebrations, spreading joy with every bite.

For those who enjoy experimenting in the kitchen, Peppermint Bark Brownies offer an opportunity to explore variations and adaptations. Including mix-ins, such as chopped nuts or dark chocolate chunks, adds complexity to the texture and flavor profile. The choice of peppermint candies, whether traditional candy canes or artisanal peppermint treats, allows for customization that suits individual preferences.

The visual appeal of Peppermint Bark Brownies can be further enhanced through creative presentation and decorating techniques. Drizzles of contrasting chocolate, a sprinkle of edible pearls, or the addition of festive sprinkles can transform each brownie into a miniature work of art. Decorating becomes a joyful expression of creativity, allowing bakers to tailor their creations to the theme of their holiday celebrations.

In conclusion, Peppermint Bark Brownies are more than a decadent treat; they celebrate the holiday spirit captured in each luxurious bite. The harmonious fusion of rich chocolate and refreshing peppermint creates a sensory experience that transcends the act of baking, inviting individuals to savor the joy of the season. Whether enjoyed as a personal indulgence, shared with loved ones, or presented as a thoughtful gift, these brownies embody the magic of the holidays in a decadent and delightful form. Peppermint Bark Brownies are not just a dessert; they are a festive tradition, a visual masterpiece, and a sweet reminder of the joy accompanying the season's celebrations.

Candy Cane Cupcakes

In the world of festive baking, Candy Cane Cupcakes stand as charming ambassadors of holiday sweetness. These delightful treats combine the familiarity of cupcakes with the notion of candy canes, creating a confection that not only captures the essence of the season but also adds a playful twist to the traditional cupcake experience. Candy Cane Cupcakes are a delightful marriage of flavors, textures, and visual appeal, making them a perfect addition to holiday celebrations and dessert tables.

The foundation of Candy Cane Cupcakes lies in the artistry of cupcake baking, a timeless tradition that invites both seasoned bakers and novices into the joyous world of homemade desserts. The process begins with carefully selecting and measuring ingredients—flour, sugar, butter, eggs, and leavening agents—crafted into a luscious batter that forms the basis of the cupcakes. This standard cupcake canvas becomes the stage upon which the magic of candy canes unfolds.

The distinctive candy cane flavor is introduced by carefully incorporating finely crushed peppermint candies into the cupcake batter. The choice of quality peppermint candies is paramount, ensuring an authentic and robust minty essence that harmonizes with the sweetness of the cupcakes. The finely crushed candies infuse the batter with peppermint flavor and create delightful speckles that add visual interest to each bite.

Baking Candy Cane Cupcakes is a sensory journey that transforms the kitchen into a festive haven. As the cupcakes rise in the oven, the delightful aroma of baking vanilla and peppermint fills the air, creating an atmosphere that encapsulates the warmth and joy of holiday baking. The anticipation builds as the cupcakes take shape, their golden tops promising a delectable treat embodying the season's spirit.

Upon emerging from the oven, Candy Cane Cupcakes reveal their visual charm. The golden-brown tops, adorned with festive red and white swirls reminiscent of candy canes, create an immediate sense of holiday whimsy. The visual appeal of these cupcakes invites admiration, making them a delightful addition to dessert displays, holiday gatherings, and festive celebrations.

The first bite of a Candy Cane Cupcake is a moment of pure delight. The initial encounter with the tender crumb, enhanced by the buttery richness of the cupcake, gives way to the refreshing burst of peppermint flavor. The marriage of sweetness and mintiness creates a harmonious balance that lingers on the palate, making each bite a joyful experience. The texture, a perfect fusion of moistness and lightness, elevates Candy Cane Cupcakes beyond the ordinary.

The decoration of Candy Cane Cupcakes extends beyond the batter, introducing an opportunity for creative expression. The crowning glory of these cupcakes often involves swirls of peppermint-infused frosting, adding a layer of flavor and visual appeal. The choice of frosting—whether buttercream, cream cheese, or a marshmallow-based concoction—allows for customization, catering to individual taste preferences and thematic considerations. Candy Cane Cupcakes become a canvas for artistic embellishments. Dusting powdered sugar, a drizzle of white chocolate, or a sprinkle of crushed candy canes enhances their visual allure, turning them into miniature works of edible art. Adding festive cupcake liners, edible glitter, or decorative toppers further personalizes these cupcakes, reflecting the baker's creativity and the spirit of the occasion.

The versatility of Candy Cane Cupcakes extends to their role in holiday celebrations. Whether served at a family gathering, in a dessert spread or presented at a festive party, these cupcakes become a delightful centerpiece that adds a touch of whimsy to the occasion. Their portions make them easily shareable, encouraging guests to enjoy the festive sweetness.

For those with a penchant for hosting holiday events, Candy Cane Cupcakes can be the star of a dessert table or a charming addition to a cupcake tower. Their visual appeal and delightful flavor make them stand out among various holiday treats, inviting guests to partake in the joy of seasonal indulgence. The vibrant red and white swirls create a festive ambiance that contributes to the holiday decor.

Candy Cane Cupcakes cater to various preferences and dietary needs, allowing for inclusivity in the joy of holiday treats. Adaptations for gluten-free or dairy-free options ensure that everyone can enjoy the whimsical delight of these cupcakes. The spirit of holiday indulgence becomes accessible to a broader audience, making these treats a thoughtful inclusion in gatherings where diverse dietary needs are considered.

In conclusion, Candy Cane Cupcakes are not just a festive dessert; they celebrate holiday joy in every swirl and bite. The peppermint infusion into the classic cupcake elevates the treat to a new level of seasonal delight. Whether enjoyed as a personal indulgence, shared with loved ones, or presented as a thoughtful gift, these cupcakes encapsulate the magic of the holidays in a whimsical and delicious form. Candy Cane Cupcakes are not just cupcakes; they are a festive tradition, a visual delight, and a sweet reminder of the joy accompanying the season's celebrations.

Peppermint Cheesecake Bites

In the realm of holiday desserts, Peppermint Cheesecake Bites emerge as miniature masterpieces that embody the perfect fusion of creamy indulgence and festive freshness. These delightful treats take the classic allure of cheesecake and infuse it with the refreshing essence of peppermint, creating a blissful symphony that captivates the palate. Peppermint Cheesecake Bites not only showcase the artistry of dessert crafting but also stand as a testament to the joyous spirit of the holiday season.

Peppermint Cheesecake Bites's core lies the art of crafting the perfect cheesecake base—a symphony of cream cheese, sugar, eggs, and vanilla extract. This decadent mixture is transformed into a velvety-smooth batter that forms the foundation for the delightful cheesecake bites. Carefully blending ingredients is crucial, ensuring a harmonious balance that results in a luscious and creamy texture, setting the stage for the infusion of peppermint flavor.

The magic begins with peppermint extract, a critical ingredient that imparts a refreshing twist to the classic cheesecake. The choice of quality peppermint extract is paramount, as it determines the depth and authenticity of the minty essence that will permeate each bite. The measured addition of peppermint extract allows for a nuanced flavor profile, where peppermint's coolness complements the cheesecake's richness without overwhelming the palate.

The creative process continues by adding finely crushed peppermint candies to the cheesecake batter. This step intensifies the peppermint flavor and introduces delightful textural contrasts. The crunchy bits of candy nestled within the creamy cheesecake create a sensory experience that elevates these bites beyond ordinary desserts. The finely crushed peppermint candies become a delightful surprise, adding both visual interest and a burst of minty freshness.

Baking Peppermint Cheesecake Bites is a culinary journey that transforms the kitchen into a sanctuary of festive aromas. As the cheesecake bites bake, the irresistible scent of vanilla and peppermint permeates the air, creating an atmosphere of warmth and holiday cheer. The anticipation builds as the cheesecake bites form, their golden tops hinting at the decadent delights that await.

Upon emerging from the oven, Peppermint Cheesecake Bites reveal their visual allure. The golden-brown tops, adorned with speckles of crushed peppermint candies, create a festive mosaic that signals the perfect balance of richness and freshness within. The miniature size of these cheesecake bites adds to their charm, making them an ideal choice for elegant dessert displays and holiday gatherings.

The first bite of a Peppermint Cheesecake Bite is a moment of sheer bliss. With its rich and creamy consistency, the initial encounter with the velvety cheesecake base gives way to the refreshing peppermint burst. The combination of flavors creates a delightful harmony, where the cool and refreshing minty notes beautifully offset the sweetness of the cheesecake. The smooth and decadent texture lingers on the palate, inviting indulgence with every bite.

The presentation of Peppermint Cheesecake Bites extends beyond their delectable taste to their visual appeal. These miniature treats can be adorned with various festive embellishments, enhancing their charm and creating a feast for the eyes. A drizzle of white chocolate, a sprinkle of edible glitter, or a dusting of powdered sugar adds a touch of elegance, turning each cheesecake bite into a work of art reflecting the season's joyous spirit.

The versatility of Peppermint Cheesecake Bites extends to their role in holiday celebrations. Their bite-sized nature makes them perfect for dessert tables, offering a delightful option alongside other festive treats. The portions make them easily shareable, encouraging guests to savor the blissful combination of creamy cheesecake and minty freshness. These bites become a delightful addition to holiday parties, family gatherings, and festive occasions.

For those who enjoy the art of dessert presentation, Peppermint Cheesecake Bites provide an opportunity for creative expression. The arrangement of these bites on elegant platters or tiered serving trays creates a visually stunning display that captures the attention of dessert enthusiasts. Incorporating thematic decorations, such as miniature candy canes or festive sprinkles, enhances the overall presentation, making these cheesecake bites a focal point of holiday dessert spreads.

The adaptability of Peppermint Cheesecake Bites to various dietary preferences ensures inclusivity in the joy of holiday indulgence. With dairy-free cream cheese alternatives and gluten-free crust options, these bites can be crafted to accommodate individuals with specific dietary needs. Saving a festive treat becomes accessible to a broader audience, ensuring everyone can partake in the season's sweetness.

In conclusion, Peppermint Cheesecake Bites are not merely a holiday dessert; they celebrate indulgence, artistry, and joy in every bite. The infusion of peppermint into the classic cheesecake elevates these bites to a festive delight that resonates with the season's spirit. Whether enjoyed as a personal indulgence, shared with loved ones, or presented as a thoughtful gift, Peppermint Cheesecake Bites embody the magic of the holidays in an elegant and delicious form. These bites are not just dessert; they are a festive tradition, a visual delight, and a sweet reminder of the joy accompanying the season's celebrations.

CHAPTER VI

Creative Twists on Peppermint Classics

Peppermint Mocha Cookies

In festive baking, Peppermint Mocha Cookies emerge as delightful ambassadors of seasonal indulgence. These cookies encapsulate the beloved flavors of peppermint and mocha, creating a harmonious fusion that delights the taste buds and evokes the joyous spirit of the holidays. With a perfect balance of richness, sweetness, and a hint of minty freshness, Peppermint Mocha Cookies stand as a testament to the artistry of holiday baking.

The journey into the creation of Peppermint Mocha Cookies begins with the selection of high-quality ingredients. The foundation of these cookies is a classic chocolate cookie dough crafted with care to achieve the ideal texture and flavor. Rich cocoa powder, premium chocolate chips, and a precise combination of flour, butter, and sugar form the base that sets the stage for the decadent infusion of peppermint and mocha.

The magic unfolds with the introduction of two-star ingredients—peppermint extract and instant coffee or espresso. These components are the heart of the Peppermint Mocha Cookies, and their careful incorporation into the cookie dough is pivotal to achieving the desired flavor profile. The peppermint extract imparts an excellent, refreshing essence that complements the richness of the chocolate. At the same time, adding instant coffee or espresso elevates the cookies with a deep, aromatic mocha undertone.

The kitchen becomes a sanctuary of enticing aromas as the Peppermint Mocha Cookies bake. The heady scent of chocolate and coffee intermingles with the refreshing notes of peppermint, creating an olfactory symphony that signals the arrival of festive delights. The anticipation builds as the cookies form in the oven, their enticing fragrance wafting through the air, beckoning all to partake in the joy of holiday baking.

Upon emerging from the oven, Peppermint Mocha Cookies reveal their visual appeal. The rich, dark hue of the chocolate cookies, studded with melty chocolate chips, sets the stage for the festive touch of crushed candy canes. The cookies are adorned with finely ground peppermint candies, adding a pop of color and a hint of minty freshness that captivates the eye. Their visual allure makes them an inviting addition to holiday dessert spreads and festive gatherings.

The first bite of a Peppermint Mocha Cookie is a sensory experience that unfolds in layers. The initial crunch gives way to a soft, chewy center, where chocolate's richness and mocha's warmth dance on the palate. The subtle coolness of peppermint emerges, providing a refreshing contrast that elevates the overall flavor profile. The symphony of tastes and textures creates a delightful, comforting, festive indulgence.

The decoration of Peppermint Mocha Cookies extends beyond their intrinsic flavors, offering an opportunity for creative expression. A drizzle of white chocolate, a sprinkle of additional crushed peppermint candies, or a dusting of cocoa powder can enhance their visual appeal. The cookies become not just a treat for the taste buds but also a canvas for festive decoration, inviting bakers to showcase their creativity and add a personalized touch.

The versatility of Peppermint Mocha Cookies lies in their adaptability to different occasions. Whether served at a holiday cookie exchange, on a festive dessert platter, or packaged as thoughtful gifts, these cookies symbolize seasonal cheer. Their nature makes them easy to share, encouraging the spirit of holiday generosity and the joy of indulging in a sweet treat.

Peppermint Mocha Cookies can take center stage as a dessert highlight for those who enjoy hosting holiday gatherings. Served on elegant platters or displayed in festive cookie tins, these cookies become a visual centerpiece that adds a touch of sophistication to the dessert table. The combination of rich chocolate, refreshing peppermint, and aromatic mocha makes them a crowd-pleaser, ensuring guests indulge in the holiday spirit with each delicious bite.

The adaptability of Peppermint Mocha Cookies extends to dietary preferences, allowing for inclusivity in the joy of holiday treats. These cookies can be crafted to accommodate various dietary needs with gluten-free flour substitutes and dairy-free chocolate options. The spirit of sharing and indulgence becomes accessible to a broader audience, ensuring everyone can partake in the season's sweetness.

In conclusion, Peppermint Mocha Cookies are more than a delightful treat; they celebrate the holiday season in every bite. The fusion of rich chocolate, refreshing peppermint, and aromatic mocha creates a sensory experience that resonates with the joyous spirit of festivities. Whether enjoyed as a personal indulgence, shared with loved ones, or presented as a heartfelt gift, Peppermint Mocha Cookies embody the magic of the holidays in an indulgent and comforting form. These cookies are not just a dessert; they are a festive tradition, a visual delight, and a sweet reminder of the joy accompanying the season's celebrations.

White Chocolate Peppermint Pretzel Cookies

In the world of holiday baking, White Chocolate Peppermint Pretzel Cookies stand as an exquisite embodiment of flavor contrasts and festive elegance. These cookies bring together the sweet creaminess of white chocolate, the savory crunch of pretzels, and the invigorating freshness of peppermint in a harmonious symphony that captivates the palate. With each bite, these cookies unfold a delightful combination of textures and tastes, making them a culinary masterpiece and a highlight of seasonal indulgence.

The journey into creating White Chocolate Peppermint Pretzel Cookies begins with carefully selecting ingredients that contribute to the cookie's distinct character. The foundation is a classic cookie dough enriched with premium white chocolate chips, creating a base that promises indulgent sweetness. Adding crushed pretzels introduces a savory and crunchy element, adding depth and contrast to the overall texture of the cookies. Finally, the infusion of peppermint extract imparts a cool and refreshing essence, elevating these cookies to a festive delight.

The magic of White Chocolate Peppermint Pretzel Cookies lies in the thoughtful incorporation of these critical elements. When melted during baking, the white chocolate chips create pockets of creamy richness that intermingle with the cookie dough. This infusion of sweetness is complemented by the crunchy texture and salty notes contributed by the crushed pretzels. The peppermint extract, carefully measured to avoid overpowering, adds a refreshing undertone that balances the sweetness and brings a festive touch to each bite.

As the cookies bake, the kitchen is filled with the enticing aromas of melting white chocolate, the toasty scent of baking cookies, and the subtle minty notes of peppermint. The symphony of fragrances creates an ambiance that invites anticipation, signaling the imminent arrival of a delightful treat. The visual transformation of the cookies, with the white chocolate melting into golden pools and the pretzel pieces adding a rustic charm, adds to the sensory appeal of these festive creations.

Upon emerging from the oven, White Chocolate Peppermint Pretzel Cookies reveal their visual allure. The golden-brown edges, studded with white chocolate chips and pretzel pieces, create a picturesque landscape that mirrors the diverse flavors within. The artful combination of colors and textures makes these cookies a delight for the taste buds and a visual feast, perfect for holiday dessert displays and festive gatherings.

The first bite of a White Chocolate Peppermint Pretzel Cookie is a revelation of contrasts. The initial crunch gives way to the soft and chewy center, where the sweetness of white chocolate harmonizes with the savory crunch of pretzels. The subtle coolness of peppermint emerges, adding a refreshing note that lingers on the palate. The combination of sweet, salty, and minty creates a complex flavor profile that makes each bite an exploration of taste and texture.

The decoration of White Chocolate Peppermint Pretzel Cookies extends beyond the baking process, offering an opportunity for creative expression. Drizzles of additional melted white chocolate, a sprinkle of crushed candy canes, or a dusting of powdered sugar can enhance their visual appeal. The cookies become not just a treat for the taste buds but also a canvas for festive decoration, inviting bakers to add a personalized touch to each creation.

The versatility of White Chocolate Peppermint Pretzel Cookies lies in their suitability for various occasions. Whether served at a holiday cookie exchange, on a festive dessert platter, or presented as gifts, these cookies symbolize seasonal indulgence. Their portions make them ideal for sharing, encouraging the spirit of holiday generosity and the joy of indulging in a sweet treat with loved ones.

White Chocolate Peppermint Pretzel Cookies can take center stage as a dessert highlight for those who revel in the joy of holiday hosting. Arranged on elegant platters or displayed in decorative cookie tins, these cookies become a visual centerpiece that adds a touch of sophistication to the dessert table. The combination of white chocolate, pretzels, and peppermint makes them crowd-pleasers, ensuring guests savor the festive spirit with every delectable bite.

The adaptability of White Chocolate Peppermint Pretzel Cookies to diverse dietary preferences ensures inclusivity in the joy of holiday treats. With gluten-free pretzels and dairy-free white chocolate options, these cookies can be crafted to accommodate various dietary needs. The spirit of sharing and indulgence becomes accessible to a broader audience, ensuring everyone can partake in the season's sweetness.

In conclusion, White Chocolate Peppermint Pretzel Cookies are not merely a holiday dessert; they celebrate indulgence, creativity, and joy in every bite. The fusion of white chocolate, pretzels, and peppermint creates a sensory experience that resonates with the festive spirit of the holidays. Whether enjoyed as a personal indulgence, shared with loved ones, or presented as a thoughtful gift, these cookies embody the magic of the season in a form that is both elegant and delicious. They are not just cookies; they are a festive tradition, a visual delight, and a sweet reminder of the joy accompanying the season's celebrations.

Peppermint Hot Cocoa Truffles

In the realm of holiday confections, Peppermint Hot Cocoa Truffles emerge as luxurious indulgences that marry the rich, velvety notes of hot cocoa with the invigorating freshness of peppermint. These truffles, with their smooth and creamy centers enveloped in a decadent chocolate shell, capture the essence of warmth and comfort synonymous with a cup of hot cocoa on a chilly winter day. With each exquisite bite, Peppermint Hot Cocoa Truffles invite a sensory journey that combines the indulgence of chocolate with the refreshing burst of mint, making them a quintessential treat for the festive season.

The artistry of Peppermint Hot Cocoa Truffles begins with the careful selection of high-quality ingredients. At the heart of these confections is a ganache made from premium chocolate, chosen for its deep, complex flavor profile. The chocolate is finely chopped and combined with heated heavy cream to create a smooth and luscious ganache that forms the silky core of each truffle. This ganache serves as the canvas upon which hot cocoa and peppermint flavors are artfully layered.

The comforting warmth of hot cocoa inspires the first layer of flavor. Cocoa powder is introduced to the ganache, imparting a rich and intense chocolate essence that harks back to the cherished ritual of sipping hot cocoa by the fireside. The careful balance of cocoa ensures that the truffles embody the essence of this beloved winter beverage, creating a nostalgic connection for those who revel in the soothing pleasure of a cup of cocoa during the holiday season.

The second layer of flavor introduces the refreshing coolness of peppermint. Peppermint extract is incorporated into the ganache, infusing it with a refreshing and minty aroma. Adding peppermint elevates the truffles, transforming them from a simple chocolate confection into a festive treat that captures the season's spirit. The careful measure of peppermint extract ensures that the minty notes are present without overpowering the delicate balance of chocolate and cream.

Crafting Peppermint Hot Cocoa Truffles becomes a sensory experience as the ganache takes shape. The aroma of melting chocolate, the deep scent of cocoa, and the refreshing whiff of peppermint create an olfactory symphony that envelops the kitchen. As the ganache cools and sets, it becomes pliable, creating perfectly portioned truffle centers that will soon be enrobed in a glossy chocolate coating.

The next phase of artistry involves coating the ganache centers with a decadent chocolate shell. The choice of chocolate for the outer layer is paramount, as it contributes to the truffle's appearance and enhances its overall flavor. High-quality dark chocolate, with its nuanced notes and smooth texture, is often preferred, creating a harmonious contrast to the creamy ganache. The careful tempering of the chocolate ensures a glossy finish and a satisfying snap as the truffle is bitten into.

As the truffles are dipped and coated, they have a polished appearance, each resembling a miniature work of art. The final step in their creation often involves sprinkling crushed candy canes or dusting cocoa powder, adding a festive touch that elevates their visual appeal. These embellishments contribute to the truffles' aesthetics and offer a hint of the flavors that await within—chocolate, mint, and the cozy warmth of hot cocoa.

The presentation of Peppermint Hot Cocoa Truffles extends beyond their visual allure to the sensory pleasure of each bite—the initial encounter with the glossy chocolate exterior yields the soft and velvety ganache within. The indulgent richness of chocolate mingles with the refreshing burst of peppermint, creating a multi-layered experience that unfolds with each moment. The truffles melt on the tongue, leaving behind a lingering symphony of flavors that evoke the joyous spirit of the holidays.

These truffles are not merely a delectable treat; they embody seasonal comfort and festive elegance. Whether enjoyed as a personal indulgence, shared with loved ones, or presented as a thoughtful gift, Peppermint Hot Cocoa Truffles evoke a sense of celebration in every bite. Their portions make them ideal for gifting, allowing recipients to savor the decadence of a luxurious chocolate experience that encapsulates the warmth and joy of the season.

For those who appreciate the art of holiday hosting, Peppermint Hot Cocoa Truffles become a delightful addition to dessert platters and festive displays. Arranged in elegant boxes or displayed on decorative trays, these truffles become a visual centerpiece that adds a touch of sophistication to the dessert table. The combination of chocolate and peppermint makes them a crowd-pleaser, ensuring that guests indulge in the decadent spirit of the season.

The adaptability of Peppermint Hot Cocoa Truffles extends to various dietary preferences, making them an inclusive delight for diverse audiences. With dairy-free chocolate and plant-based cream alternatives, these truffles can be crafted to accommodate individuals with specific dietary needs. The joy of savoring a luxurious chocolate experience becomes accessible to a broader audience, ensuring everyone can partake in the season's sweetness. In conclusion, Peppermint Hot Cocoa Truffles are more than a confection; they celebrate indulgence, craftsmanship, and the quintessential flavors of the holidays. The marriage of rich chocolate, comforting hot cocoa, and refreshing peppermint creates a sensory experience that resonates with the season's festive spirit. Whether enjoyed in quiet moments of personal reflection or shared in the company of others, these truffles embody the magic of the holidays in a decadent and heartwarming form. They are not just truffles; they are a festive tradition, a visual delight, and a sweet reminder of the joy accompanying the season's celebrations.

CHAPTER VII

Gluten-Free and Vegan Peppermint Options

Exploring Gluten-Free Peppermint Treats

The culinary landscape has witnessed a remarkable evolution in recent years, with an increasing emphasis on accommodating diverse dietary needs. For those who adhere to a gluten-free lifestyle, the quest for delectable treats that meet dietary restrictions and flavor expectations can be challenging. However, the world of gluten-free baking has undergone a transformative journey, and within it, a delightful array of Peppermint Treats has emerged, offering a decadent experience without compromise.

At the heart of this exploration lies the commitment to crafting gluten-free versions of beloved peppermint-infused confections. Whether it be cookies, cakes, or truffles, the challenge is met with creativity, innovation, and a dedication to ensuring that every bite is a celebration of flavors. Gluten-free Peppermint Treats not only cater to those with dietary restrictions but also stand as a testament to the culinary artistry that transcends the boundaries of traditional baking.

The foundation of gluten-free Peppermint Treats is carefully selecting alternative flours and starches. Almond flour, coconut flour, and gluten-free all-purpose flour blends step into the spotlight, providing a structure that mirrors the texture of their gluten-containing counterparts. The nuanced flavors of these alternative flours contribute to the complexity of the treats, enhancing rather than compromising the overall taste experience.

In gluten-free Peppermint Cookies, almond flour often takes center stage. The finely ground almonds impart a delicate nuttiness that harmonizes with the refreshing coolness of peppermint. These cookies, whether in the form of sheer cutouts or chewy drops, redefine the expectations of gluten-free baking, offering a satisfyingly crisp and delightfully tender texture.

The journey extends to gluten-free Peppermint Cakes, where a blend of gluten-free flours creates a moist and flavorful crumb. The challenge lies in achieving the desired lightness and fluffiness without the structure provided by traditional wheat flour. Through carefully chosen gluten-free flour blends and additional leavening agents, bakers embark on a quest to create cakes that rise to the occasion in terms of taste and texture.

Peppermint Truffles, a decadent indulgence in the world of confections, also undergo a gluten-free transformation. The luscious ganache at the core of these truffles relies on gluten-free chocolate and dairy alternatives to achieve the desired richness. The absence of gluten does not equate to a compromise in flavor or texture; instead, it opens doors to a realm of possibilities where the interplay of chocolate and peppermint takes center stage.

The introduction of gluten-free Peppermint Treats to the holiday dessert repertoire extends beyond mere adaptation; it is a celebration of inclusivity and the acknowledgment that dietary restrictions should not limit the joy of indulging in festive delights. As gluten-free baking becomes more sophisticated and widely embraced, the options for creating Peppermint Treats that cater to diverse palates continue to expand.

One of the critical challenges in gluten-free baking is achieving the desired texture and structure without gluten —a protein that provides elasticity and structure in traditional baked goods. However, innovative combinations of alternative flours, starches, and binding agents rise to the occasion, creating treats that defy expectations and showcase the versatility of gluten-free baking.

The success of gluten-free Peppermint Treats is not solely reliant on choosing flours; it also hinges on carefully selecting additional ingredients. Using high-quality chocolate, premium peppermint extract, and natural sweeteners ensures that the treats maintain a standard of excellence. The incorporation of other flavor enhancers, such as vanilla, enhances the overall taste profile, creating treats that are indulgent, flavorful, and free from gluten.

The exploration of gluten-free Peppermint Treats is not confined to traditional recipes; it extends to innovative creations that push the boundaries of conventional baking. From gluten-free Peppermint Cheesecake Bars to Flourless Peppermint Chocolate Torte, bakers are continually pushing the envelope to deliver treats that meet dietary restrictions and surpass expectations in terms of taste and presentation.

With its myriad of festive flavors, the holiday season serves as the perfect canvas for gluten-free Peppermint Treats to shine. Whether served at a holiday gathering, shared at a cookie exchange, or presented as a thoughtful gift, these treats symbolize inclusion and the joy of seasonal indulgence. The commitment to gluten-free baking is not just a culinary endeavor but an affirmation that everyone, regardless of dietary restrictions, deserves to partake in the season's sweetness.

The appeal of gluten-free Peppermint Treats goes beyond the gluten-sensitive community; it resonates with a broader audience seeking flavorful and diverse options. As awareness of gluten-free alternatives grows, these treats become a choice rather than a compromise. The ability to cater to various dietary needs adds a layer of accessibility to holiday desserts, ensuring that the joy of indulgence is inclusive and shared by all.

For those who embark on crafting gluten-free Peppermint Treats, it is a labor of love that extends beyond baking. It is an expression of creativity, a commitment to providing options for those with dietary restrictions, and a celebration of the diverse flavors that contribute to the richness of the holiday season. The evolution of gluten-free baking has transformed Peppermint Treats into a culinary art form that invites everyone to savor the magic of the holidays, bite by delicious gluten-free bite.

In conclusion, the exploration of gluten-free Peppermint Treats represents a culinary triumph that goes beyond adaptation and transcends limitations. It is a celebration of diversity, flavor, and the inclusive spirit of the holiday season. Gluten-free baking has evolved from a niche endeavor to mainstream culinary art, and Peppermint Treats have emerged as a delightful testament to the fact that decadence knows no bounds. Whether enjoyed by those with gluten sensitivities or by enthusiasts seeking a flavorful twist, these treats redefine the holiday dessert experience, proving that indulgence can be both gluten-free and utterly delicious.

Vegan Peppermint Delicacies

In the evolving landscape of culinary delights, vegan baking has undergone a revolutionary transformation, dispelling any notion that plant-based treats lack the indulgence and decadence of traditional desserts. Within this paradigm, Vegan Peppermint Delicacies emerge as exquisite creations that celebrate the harmonious marriage of plant-based ingredients with the invigorating freshness of peppermint. These delicacies, ranging from cookies and cakes to truffles and beyond, not only cater to a vegan lifestyle but also stand as a testament to the creativity and artistry that flourishes in plant-based baking.

Vegan Peppermint Delicacies' core is the mindful selection of ingredients that eschew animal products without compromising taste and texture. Plant-based alternatives such as coconut oil, nut butter, and non-dairy milk become the building blocks of these treats, offering a rich and nuanced flavor profile that rivals their traditional counterparts. The use of whole foods, such as nuts and seeds, further contributes to the nutritional depth of these creations.

In Vegan Peppermint Cookies, the absence of dairy and eggs does not hinder the creation of melt-in-your-mouth delights. Coconut oil and nut butter are luscious replacements, imparting a subtle nuttiness that complements the peppermint infusion. These cookies, whether soft and chewy or delicately crispy, showcase the versatility of plant-based ingredients in achieving the desired textures that evoke a sense of indulgence.
Vegan Peppermint Cakes, a pinnacle of plant-based baking, boast moist and flavorful crumbs without the reliance on butter or eggs. The creativity in vegan cake recipes lies in using ingredients like applesauce, flax eggs, or mashed bananas as binding agents and moisture enhancers. These cakes, adorned with the refreshing coolness of peppermint, redefine the expectations of plant-based desserts, proving that vegan treats can be as sumptuous and celebratory as their non-vegan counterparts.

The artistry extends to Vegan Peppermint Truffles, where plant-based alternatives to heavy cream and dairy chocolate transform the ganache into a creamy masterpiece. The interplay of coconut cream, avocado, or nut-based alternatives ensures a rich, velvety texture that rivals traditional truffles. The absence of dairy does not diminish indulgence; instead, it opens doors to a world of innovative combinations that elevate these truffles to a level of plant-based decadence.

The introduction of Vegan Peppermint Delicacies to the holiday dessert repertoire is a celebration of plant-based living and the rich tapestry of flavors woven from ingredients sourced from the plant kingdom. Vegan baking transcends the boundaries of dietary choices and becomes a celebration of mindful eating, sustainability, and cruelty-free indulgence.

One of the critical challenges in vegan baking lies in replacing the role of eggs and dairy, which contribute not only to the structure but also to the moisture and richness of traditional baked goods. However, the vegan baking community has unlocked a treasure trove of possibilities through experimentation with plant-based alternatives. Aquafaba, the liquid from canned chickpeas, becomes a magical substitute for egg whites. At the same time, nut butter and fruit purees stand in for butter and eggs, creating a symphony of flavors and textures that delight vegan baking.

The success of Vegan Peppermint Delicacies hinges on the quality of the ingredients chosen. The use of high-quality non-dairy chocolate, premium peppermint extract, and natural sweeteners ensures that the treats maintain a standard of excellence. The incorporation of other flavor enhancers, such as citrus zest or herbal infusions, adds layers of complexity to the overall taste profile, creating treats that are not only vegan but also vibrant and indulgent.

Exploring Vegan Peppermint Delicacies extends beyond replicating traditional recipes to creating innovative and trend-setting treats. From Vegan Peppermint

Cheesecakes with nut-based crusts to Flourless Chocolate Peppermint Brownies, vegan bakers continually push the boundaries of plant-based desserts, proving that indulgence knows no limitations.

With its palette of festive flavors, the holiday season provides the perfect canvas for Vegan Peppermint Delicacies to shine. Whether served at a plant-based feast, shared at a holiday gathering, or presented as a thoughtful gift, these treats symbolize compassion, sustainability, and the joy of seasonal indulgence. The commitment to vegan baking is not just a culinary endeavor but an affirmation that everyone, regardless of their dietary choices, deserves to partake in the season's sweetness.

The appeal of Vegan Peppermint Delicacies extends beyond the vegan community; it resonates with a broader audience seeking flavorful and diverse options. As plant-based living becomes more mainstream, these treats become a choice rather than a compromise. The ability to cater to various dietary preferences adds a layer of inclusivity to holiday desserts, ensuring that all share the joy of indulgence.

For those who craft Vegan Peppermint Delicacies, it is a celebration of culinary innovation, a commitment to sustainability, and a joyful exploration of the vibrant flavors offered by plant-based ingredients. The evolution of vegan baking has transformed Peppermint Delicacies into a culinary art form that invites everyone to savor the magic of the holidays, one compassionate and indulgent bite at a time.

In conclusion, the exploration of Vegan Peppermint Delicacies represents a culinary triumph that goes beyond meeting dietary preferences to redefine the expectations of plant-based indulgence. It is a celebration of diversity, flavor, and the inclusive spirit of the holiday season. Vegan baking has evolved from a niche endeavor to mainstream culinary art. Peppermint Delicacies have emerged as a delightful testament to the fact that decadence can be both vegan and utterly delicious.

Inclusive Peppermint Baking for All

As the culinary landscape evolves, inclusivity becomes a central theme in baking. The once-narrow definition of traditional treats is expanding to accommodate diverse dietary needs and preferences, ushering in an era where everyone can enjoy creating and savoring delightful confections. With its refreshing coolness and festive allure, Peppermint baking takes center stage in this inclusive revolution, inviting individuals of all backgrounds and dietary choices to indulge in a symphony of flavors that transcends traditional boundaries.

At the heart of inclusive peppermint baking lies the recognition that diversity is not just a reflection of personal choices but a celebration of the richness that emerges when various culinary traditions and dietary needs converge. Whether one follows a gluten-free, vegan, or traditional diet, the goal is to create a space in the kitchen where everyone can contribute to and partake in the joy of baking without compromise.

In the realm of inclusive peppermint baking, the journey begins with exploring alternative flours for those seeking gluten-free options. Almond flour, coconut flour, and gluten-free all-purpose blends step into the spotlight, offering a canvas upon which the nuanced flavors of peppermint can be artfully expressed. The result is a collection of gluten-free peppermint cookies, cakes, and truffles that redefine expectations, proving that indulgence knows no bounds.

For those embracing a vegan lifestyle, the emphasis shifts to plant-based alternatives that replace dairy and eggs while preserving the decadence of traditional treats.

Coconut oil, nut butter, and non-dairy milk become the building blocks for vegan peppermint cookies and cakes, showcasing the versatility of ingredients sourced from the plant kingdom. The result is a delectable array of vegan peppermint delicacies that stand alongside their non-vegan counterparts, ensuring that no one is excluded from the pleasures of the holiday table.

The inclusive spirit of peppermint baking extends to those with specific dietary needs, such as gluten sensitivities or lactose intolerance. The availability of gluten- and dairy-free alternatives broadens the scope of traditional recipes and empowers individuals to tailor their baking adventures to meet their unique requirements. In this inclusive kitchen, the joy of creating and sharing peppermint treats becomes a shared experience, transcending dietary restrictions to focus on celebrating flavors.

A key aspect of inclusive peppermint baking is acknowledging that the holiday season is a time for communal joy, and no one should feel excluded from the festivities. Traditional recipes are revisited and adapted to accommodate diverse dietary preferences, ensuring that the dessert table becomes a space where everyone can find a treat that resonates with their tastes and values.

Traditional peppermint baking also receives its due attention in the spirit of inclusivity. Classic recipes for gingerbread cutouts, houses, and peppermint bark find their place alongside their gluten-free and vegan counterparts, creating a harmonious blend that caters to a spectrum of tastes and dietary choices. The inclusive kitchen becomes a space where the essence of tradition coexists with the innovation of modern adaptations, offering a holistic and diverse culinary experience. Inclusive

peppermint baking is about accommodating dietary needs and fostering an environment where everyone feels welcome and valued. The kitchen becomes a space for creative expression, a canvas where individuals can share their unique perspectives and contribute to a collective celebration of flavors. In this inclusive realm, bakers are not bound by rigid definitions of tradition but are free to explore, experiment, and reimagine peppermint-infused delights that resonate with their preferences.

As the inclusive peppermint baking movement gains momentum, it extends beyond the confines of individual kitchens to embrace the larger community. Recipes are shared, adapted, and celebrated in a communal exchange that transcends geographical and cultural boundaries. Social media platforms become a virtual space where bakers from around the world showcase their inclusive peppermint creations, fostering a global conversation that celebrates the diversity of tastes and traditions.

The inclusive peppermint baking movement also emphasizes education and awareness. Resources and guides for gluten-free and vegan baking techniques become readily available, empowering individuals to embark on inclusive baking journeys. The goal is to provide recipes and share knowledge, tips, and tricks that make the world of inclusive baking accessible to all.

In conclusion, inclusive peppermint baking is a celebration of diversity, a culinary movement that invites everyone to the table, regardless of their dietary choices or restrictions. It is a recognition that the joy of baking and savoring delicious treats should be a shared experience that transcends traditional boundaries. Inclusive peppermint baking is not just about the final product; it is about the journey, the creativity, and the collective celebration of flavors that make the holiday season a time of joy and inclusivity for all.

CHAPTER VIII

Perfecting Peppermint Decorations

Royal Icing Masterclass for Peppermint-Themed Cookies

In the realm of festive baking, the allure of peppermint-themed cookies transcends the ordinary, inviting bakers to embark on a journey of creativity and flavor. At the heart of crafting these edible masterpieces lies the art of royal icing—a versatile and transformative medium that serves as the canvas for intricate designs and enhances the flavor profile of the cookies. This royal icing masterclass celebrates the craftsmanship, precision, and artistry that elevate peppermint-themed cookies to a level of sophistication that captivates both the eyes and the taste buds.

The canvas for this masterclass is the humble sugar cookie, a blank slate eagerly awaiting the touch of royal icing artistry. The foundation of any tremendous peppermint-themed cookie is a perfectly baked sugar cookie—crisp at the edges, tender at the center, and a harmonious blend of sweetness and vanilla undertones. This classic canvas becomes the stage upon which the magic of royal icing unfolds.

The journey begins with preparing the royal icing—a mixture of confectioners' sugar, meringue powder, and water. The key to achieving the perfect consistency lies in the delicate balance of these ingredients. A stiff consistency is required to outline the cookie's shape and create defined borders, while a flood consistency, achieved by thinning the icing with water, fills the outlined areas seamlessly. The result is a smooth, glossy surface that serves as the backdrop for intricate peppermint- inspired designs.

Peppermint-themed cookies are a celebration of both flavor and aesthetics. The infusion of peppermint extract into the royal icing adds a layer of freshness that complements the cookie's sweetness. The intensity of the peppermint flavor can be adjusted to suit individual preferences, creating a symphony of taste that mirrors the visual artistry of the designs. The royal icing becomes not merely a decorative element but an integral part of the overall flavor experience.

One of the critical techniques in royal icing masterclass is the art of flooding—filling the outlined areas with thinned icing to create a smooth and seamless surface. This technique requires precision and patience as the flood-consistency icing is guided into place using piping bags or squeeze bottles. The result is a beautifully coated cookie that provides the perfect canvas for additional detailing.

The palette of colors in a royal icing masterclass is as diverse as the imagination allows. Peppermint-themed cookies often feature a traditional color scheme of red and white, reminiscent of candy canes and the season's festive spirit. Achieving vibrant and consistent colors involves using gel food coloring, allowing for precise control over the shade and intensity of each hue. The ability to create gradients, ombre effects, and intricate patterns showcases the versatility of royal icing as an artistic medium.

The masterclass extends beyond the basic techniques of flooding and outlining to explore the world of dimensional royal icing decorations. Three-dimensional elements such as rosettes, bows, and even miniature peppermint candies can be crafted separately and affixed to the cookies once the base layer has dried. This layering of dimensions adds depth and visual interest to the cookies, transforming them from simple treats to edible works of art.

Beyond the technical aspects, the royal icing masterclass delves into the realm of storytelling through cookies. Peppermint-themed cookies can evoke a sense of nostalgia, capturing the essence of holiday traditions and childhood memories. Whether it be a snowflake, a candy cane, or a whimsical winter scene, each cookie becomes a miniature masterpiece that tells a story and elicits a heartfelt response from those who partake in its beauty.

The masterclass also explores the delicate balance between artistry and accessibility. While intricate designs and detailed piping can be awe-inspiring, the joy of royal icing is that it accommodates all skill levels. Bakers can start with simple designs and gradually progress to more complex creations as their confidence and proficiency grow. The emphasis is on the joy of the process and the sense of accomplishment that comes with creating something beautiful and delicious.

The royal icing masterclass extends its influence to texture, introducing techniques such as marbling, stenciling, and brush embroidery. Marbling involves swirling different colored icings together to create a mesmerizing visual effect, while stenciling allows intricate patterns to transfer onto the cookies. Brush embroidery, a delicate technique miming the appearance of embroidery stitches, adds elegance and whimsy to the designs.

In the spirit of inclusivity, the masterclass also explores alternative sweeteners and royal icing variations for those with dietary restrictions. Using natural sweeteners, such as maple syrup or agave nectar, provides a healthier option without compromising the integrity of the icing. Additionally, vegan royal icing recipes replace traditional meringue powder with aquafaba or other plant-based alternatives, ensuring that all can experience the joy of peppermint-themed cookies.

A crucial aspect of the royal icing masterclass is the exploration of troubleshooting and problem-solving. Bakers may encounter issues such as icing consistency, air bubbles, or bleeding colors. The masterclass provides insights into identifying and addressing these challenges, empowering bakers to navigate the intricacies of royal icing confidently.

The masterclass also delves into the proper storage and packaging of royal icing-decorated cookies. Once the icing has thoroughly dried and set, cookies should be stored in a cool, dry place to maintain freshness and prevent any potential bleeding or smudging of the designs. Thoughtful packaging, whether for personal enjoyment or gifting, ensures that the cookies remain a visual delight until they are ready to be savored.

In conclusion, the royal icing masterclass for peppermint-themed cookies is a journey into the intersection of artistry and flavor. It celebrates the transformative power of royal icing as a creative medium, allowing bakers to bring their visions to life on a delectable canvas. The masterclass is an invitation to explore, experiment, and revel in the joy of creating edible masterpieces that captivate the eyes and tantalize the taste buds. Whether crafting simple designs or intricate works of art, the royal icing masterclass is a testament to the enchanting world of festive baking, where every cookie becomes a unique expression of art and flavor.

Creative Decorating Tips for Peppermint Treats

In the enchanting realm of holiday baking, peppermint treats stand as a timeless symbol of festive joy. Beyond the delectable flavors, it is the art of creative decorating that transforms these treats into edible masterpieces, inviting both bakers and admirers on a visual and gastronomic journey. From cookies and cakes to truffles and more, the canvas for creative expression knows no bounds. This exploration of decorating tips for peppermint treats celebrates ingenuity, a guide that unveils the secrets to transforming simple confections into visually stunning and irresistibly tempting delights.

The foundation of creative decorating begins with selecting peppermint treats that serve as the blank canvas for artistic expression. Sugar cookies, gingerbread, and chocolate truffles are popular choices, each offering a unique texture and flavor profile that can be enhanced by thoughtful decoration. Whether it be the classic sugar cookie, a soft and chewy gingerbread creation, or the velvety richness of a chocolate truffle, the chosen treat sets the stage for a symphony of creativity.

Color plays a pivotal role in the visual appeal of peppermint treats, and the classic pairing of red and white evokes the traditional spirit of the season. Gel food coloring provides vibrant hues that can be expertly blended to create gradients, ombre effects, and intricate patterns. For a modern twist, consider introducing unexpected colors like mint green or icy blue to add a touch of whimsy to the traditional palette. The key is to let the colors evoke the peppermint theme and convey a sense of joy and celebration.

Texture is an often overlooked but crucial element in creative decorating. The addition of textured elements introduces depth and visual interest to peppermint treats. For sugar cookies, experiment with embossing rolling pins or textured mats to imprint festive patterns onto the dough before baking. Royal icing can create intricate patterns, such as swirls or snowflakes, adding a tactile dimension to the visual experience. Edible glitter or shimmer dust is another tool that imparts a touch of magic, catching the light and transforming treats into sparkling delights.

Experimenting with different piping tips opens up a world of possibilities in creative decorating. Consider using fine-tipped piping bags to create delicate lines and intricate details for peppermint-themed cookies. A small round tip is ideal for outlining shapes and adding finer details, while a star tip can be employed to develop rosettes or decorative borders. The choice of tip not only influences the appearance of the treat but also determines the texture of the icing, from smooth and glossy to intricately textured.

Dimensional decorations add a whimsical touch to peppermint treats, turning them into miniature works of edible art. For sugar cookies, fondant can be rolled out and cut into festive shapes, providing a smooth and pliable surface for intricate designs. Fondant decorations can be affixed to the cookies using a dab of royal icing, creating a seamless and visually appealing finish—experiment with layering fondant pieces to create depth, such as stacking fondant snowflakes or peppermint candies.

In the world of gingerbread creations, three-dimensional decorations reach new heights. Building upon the traditional gingerbread house, consider constructing a winter wonderland with gingerbread trees, snowmen, and even miniature sleighs. Royal icing serves as an adhesive and a medium for creating snow-like textures on rooftops and landscapes. The incorporation of edible elements such as shredded coconut or sanding sugar adds a touch of realism to the wintry scene.

Chocolate truffles, with their luscious centers and decadent coatings, offer a canvas for flavor and decoration. Experiment with different coatings, such as crushed candy canes, chopped nuts, or drizzles of contrasting chocolate. The key is to create a visual contrast that enhances the truffle's appearance and complements the peppermint flavor. Consider dusting the truffles with cocoa powder or edible gold dust for an elegant touch.

When it comes to truffles, presentation is as important as taste. Creative decorating extends to the packaging and serving of these delectable delights. Elegant gift boxes, festive tins, or even miniature jars adorned with ribbons and tags elevate the truffles from a simple confection to a thoughtful and visually pleasing gift. Consider experimenting with various packaging materials, such as translucent cellophane or festive fabric, to add an extra layer of sophistication.

For an interactive and engaging experience, consider hosting a peppermint decorating party. Provide array decorating tools, from piping bags and sprinkles to edible markers and fondant, allowing guests to unleash their creativity. Various treat options, including cookies, cupcakes, and truffles, ensure that everyone can find a canvas that resonates with their artistic vision. The shared experience of decorating adds an element of joy and creates lasting memories.

The possibilities for creative decorating are limitless in the realm of peppermint-themed cakes. Experiment with different cake shapes and sizes to create a festive centerpiece that captures the season's spirit. Fondant becomes a versatile medium for shaping intricate designs, from peppermint swirls to miniature presents. The art of stacking and layering cakes allows for the creation of visually stunning tiered masterpieces that serve as both a feast for the eyes and a delectable dessert.

Creative decorating extends beyond the visual to engage the sense of smell. Infusing peppermint extract into the decorating elements, such as royal icing or fondant, ensures that the treats look delightful and exude the refreshing aroma of peppermint. This multisensory experience adds a layer of delight, making the treats even more enticing and festive.

Experimenting with flavor profiles is a creative decorating tip that transcends traditional boundaries. Consider incorporating unexpected flavors like citrus zest into royal icing or testing with flavored extracts like vanilla or almond. The interplay of diverse flavors adds complexity to the treats, creating a taste experience that goes beyond the expected. Explore complementary flavors such as chocolate-orange or raspberry-peppermint for an adventurous twist, creating a delightful fusion of tastes.

Embracing the whimsical side of creative decorating, consider incorporating edible shapes and figures into peppermint treats. Marzipan or modeling chocolate can be sculpted into charming characters, such as snowmen or polar bears, adding a touch of playfulness to the treats. Edible gold or silver leaf can highlight specific elements, creating a sense of opulence and luxury.

Experimenting with unconventional shapes and forms is a creative decorating tip that adds an element of surprise to peppermint treats. Instead of traditional round truffles, consider shaping them into miniature peppermint swirls or festive holiday symbols. For cookies, explore cookie cutters in unique shapes, such as snowflakes, mittens, or even holiday-themed characters. The unexpected shapes add an element of intrigue and individuality to the treats.

In conclusion, the world of creative decorating for peppermint treats is a canvas of endless possibilities. It is an invitation to explore, experiment, and infuse a personal touch into every confection. From intricate designs and three-dimensional elements to unexpected flavors and textures, creative decorating elevates peppermint treats from simple delights to captivating edible art. Whether shared with loved ones or presented as thoughtful gifts, these creatively adorned treats become a celebration of the season—a feast for the eyes and a symphony of flavors that captures the magic of the holidays.

Personalizing Your Peppermint Creations

In holiday baking, the art of personalization transforms peppermint creations into more than just festive treats— they reflect individual tastes, memories, and traditions. Personalizing peppermint creations is an opportunity to infuse a unique identity into each confection, turning a batch of cookies or a decadent cake into a canvas for self- expression. This section explores how bakers can infuse their personality into peppermint delights, from selecting flavors and shapes to incorporating sentimental elements, creating an experience that transcends the ordinary and resonates with personal significance.

At the heart of personalization lies the choice of flavors—

a culinary journey that reflects individual preferences and evokes cherished memories. While the classic combination of peppermint and chocolate is a timeless favorite, the art of personalization invites bakers to explore unexpected flavor pairings. Infusing the peppermint creations with hints of citrus, such as orange or lemon zest, adds a bright and refreshing twist. For those seeking a decadent experience, experimenting with complementary flavors like coffee, caramel, or exotic spices can elevate the peppermint treats to new heights. Personalization through flavor allows bakers to create confections that celebrate the festive season and resonate with their unique taste profiles.

The canvas for personalization extends beyond flavors to

peppermint creations' every shape and form. Cookie cutters become the tools for shaping an edible narrative, allowing bakers to explore many possibilities. Traditional shapes like candy canes, snowflakes, and gingerbread men evoke a sense of nostalgia, while unique and unconventional forms—perhaps inspired by personal interests or holiday memories—add a touch of individuality. The choice of shape becomes a personal statement, transforming each creation into a tangible expression of the baker's personality.

One avenue for personalizing peppermint creations is the exploration of textures and layers. The interplay of textures adds depth and complexity to the treats, creating a multisensory experience. For cookies, experimenting with various levels of crispness or softness provides a tactile element that engages the palate. Layering different flavors and fillings in cakes, cupcakes, or truffles offers a delightful surprise with every bite. The art of personalization through texture ensures that each confection is visually appealing and a symphony of sensations that cater to individual preferences.

Color becomes a powerful tool for personalization, allowing bakers to express their creativity and style. While the classic red and white color scheme is synonymous with peppermint treats, personalization encourages the exploration of a broader palette. Adventurous bakers may opt for unconventional colors like pastel hues or metallic shades, creating a visually stunning and contemporary aesthetic. The choice of color can also be influenced by personal preferences, holiday themes, or even cultural significance, infusing each creation with layers of meaning beyond the surface.

In the realm of personalization, the art of storytelling takes center stage. Peppermint creations become a canvas for bakers to weave narratives and share personal stories with each delicious bite. For instance, a baker may incorporate family recipes or cultural traditions into the creation process, infusing the treats with a sense of heritage and identity. Decorating cookies with symbols that hold sentimental value, such as initials, milestones, or even miniature representations of cherished memories, transforms each confection into a vessel of personal significance. The act of personalization becomes a form of edible storytelling, allowing bakers to share a piece of themselves with those who partake in their creations.

Incorporating personalized messages adds an intimate touch to peppermint creations, turning them into thoughtful gifts or expressions of affection. Whether using edible ink to write festive greetings on cookies or embedding personalized messages in chocolate truffles, the power of words enhances the personalization process. Messages can convey love, gratitude, or humor, connecting the baker and the recipient beyond taste. Personalization through messages elevates peppermint treats to the realm of heartfelt gestures, making them delicious and deeply meaningful.

Another avenue for personalization is the exploration of dietary preferences and restrictions. With an increasing awareness of diverse nutritional needs, personalizing peppermint creations to accommodate specific requirements is an inclusive approach to holiday baking. Whether adapting recipes to be gluten-free, vegan, or incorporating alternative sweeteners, personalization ensures that everyone can partake in the joy of festive treats. Catering to individual dietary needs becomes a gesture of thoughtfulness, allowing bakers to share the joy of peppermint creations with a broad and diverse audience.

Incorporating elements of nostalgia into peppermint creations is a poignant form of personalization. Bakers may draw inspiration from cherished holiday memories, childhood favorites, or family traditions to infuse their creations with warmth and familiarity. Recreating a beloved family recipe or incorporating ingredients that evoke a specific memory—such as the scent of a grandparent's kitchen—creates a connection to the past that is both personal and heartwarming. Personalization through nostalgia transcends the act of baking, becoming a form of time travel that brings the essence of cherished moments into the present.

Using personal flair in presentation enhances the overall personalization of peppermint treats. Packaging becomes an extension of the baker's creativity, offering an opportunity to showcase individual style and thoughtfulness. Thoughtfully chosen gift boxes, ribbons, and tags transform a batch of cookies or truffles into a visually stunning and personalized gift. The attention to detail in the presentation reflects the baker's commitment to creating an experience beyond the taste buds.

In the realm of cakes, personalization extends to the design and decoration of elaborate centerpieces. Whether crafting a tiered cake adorned with intricate fondant details or a whimsical gingerbread house, the choice of design becomes a form of personal expression. Bakers can draw inspiration from private interests, hobbies, or even cultural symbols, turning the cake into a reflection of their individuality. Including personalized cake toppers featuring names, dates, or particular messages adds a finishing touch that elevates the creation into a piece of edible art.

For those seeking an interactive and collaborative form of personalization, hosting a peppermint decorating party becomes a festive occasion that brings friends and family together. Bakers of all ages can participate in the creation process, decorating cookies, cupcakes, or truffles according to their tastes and preferences. The shared personalization experience becomes a bonding activity that fosters a sense of community and joy, creating lasting memories for all involved.

Personalizing peppermint creations is not limited to the kitchen—it extends to the broader celebration of holiday traditions. Incorporating personalized treats into festive gatherings, whether as a dessert centerpiece or thoughtful party favors, adds a touch of individuality to the overall holiday experience. Peppermint creations become integral to the holiday tableau, a culinary expression of personal style and the season's spirit.

In conclusion, personalizing peppermint creations is an art that transcends the act of baking. It is an opportunity for bakers to infuse their unique identity, tastes, and memories into each confection, creating an experience that is visually and gastronomically delightful and deeply personal. From selecting flavors and shapes to incorporating sentimental elements, personalization transforms peppermint treats into a celebration of individuality. As bakers embark on this culinary journey of self-expression, each creation becomes a testament to the holiday season's joy, warmth, and creativity.

CHAPTER IX

Peppermint for Special Occasions

Peppermint Wedding Cookies

In the world of weddings, every detail contributes to the symphony of love and celebration that defines the special day. Among the myriad choices couples make, selecting wedding favors plays a pivotal role in expressing gratitude to guests and leaving them with lasting memories. With their delightful blend of festive flavors and elegant presentation, Peppermint wedding cookies have emerged as a charming and delectable choice for couples seeking a sweet addition to their nuptial festivities. This essay explores the enchanting world of peppermint wedding cookies, from their symbolism and flavor profiles to creative presentations and the thoughtful integration of the couple's unique love story.

The choice of peppermint as a central theme for wedding cookies holds a special significance. Peppermint is often associated with joy, warmth, and festivity—qualities that mirror the sentiments of a wedding celebration. The crisp and refreshing flavor of peppermint adds a delightful twist to traditional wedding desserts, infusing them with a touch of whimsy and seasonal charm. Incorporating peppermint into wedding cookies becomes a conscious choice to evoke a sense of celebration and create a memorable culinary experience for guests.

One of the most enchanting aspects of peppermint wedding cookies is their visual appeal. The classic red and white color palette synonymous with peppermint treats aligns seamlessly with the festive atmosphere of a wedding. The cookies can be shaped into elegant forms, such as hearts, wedding bells, or even the couple's initials, adding a personalized touch to the presentation. Royal icing allows for intricate detailing and delicate designs, transforming each cookie into a miniature edible art. Peppermint wedding cookies, arranged in decorative boxes or displayed on tiered trays, become a visually stunning element of the wedding décor, contributing to the overall aesthetic and creating a sense of anticipation for the sweet treat that awaits each guest.

Flavor profiles are crucial when selecting wedding favors, and peppermint offers a versatile and universally beloved option. The combination of peppermint and chocolate is a classic pairing that appeals to many palates. Peppermint wedding cookies can take various forms, from delicate sugar cookies with a peppermint-infused glaze to rich chocolate cookies with peppermint pieces. The balance of sweet and refreshing flavors creates a harmonious taste experience, making the cookies a delightful indulgence for guests. For couples looking to add a personal touch, experimenting with additional flavor elements—such as citrus zest, vanilla, or even a hint of spice—creates a unique and memorable treat.

Beyond their delectable taste, peppermint wedding cookies hold symbolic significance that resonates with the themes of marriage. Peppermint is often associated with sentiments of goodwill, prosperity, and positive energy, making it a fitting choice for celebrating love. The crisp and refreshing nature of peppermint reflects the fresh start and new beginnings that weddings symbolize. In many cultures, peppermint is believed to bring good luck, making it a promising choice for a token of appreciation for wedding guests. Gifting peppermint wedding cookies becomes a gesture of warmth and positive wishes, inviting guests to partake in the joyous spirit of the occasion.

The presentation of peppermint wedding cookies offers endless possibilities for creative expression. From intricately decorated individual cookies to elegantly arranged assortments, the packaging becomes a canvas for conveying the couple's style and personality. Customized cookie boxes or bags adorned with the wedding date, the couple's names, or even a heartfelt message add a personal touch to the favors. Couples may choose to align the packaging with the overall theme of the wedding, incorporating colors, motifs, or symbols that hold significance for them. The thoughtful presentation of peppermint wedding cookies transforms them from mere confections into cherished keepsakes that guests can savor and remember long after the wedding day has passed.

Incorporating the couple's unique love story into the theme of peppermint wedding cookies adds an extra layer of personalization. The cookies become a sweet treat and a narrative of the couple's journey. For example, if peppermint played a significant role in the couple's early dates or proposal, highlighting this aspect in the flavor or design of the cookies adds sentimental value. Including symbols or motifs that hold special meaning for the couple—perhaps the location of their first meeting or an emblem representing their shared interests—creates a sense of intimacy and connection. Infusing the love story into the theme of peppermint wedding cookies becomes a beautiful way to share the couple's narrative with those who are part of their celebration.

Peppermint wedding cookies also allow couples to engage in do-it-yourself (DIY) projects or collaborate with local bakers and confectioners. Couples with a passion for baking may embark on the delightful journey of creating their peppermint wedding cookies, infusing each step with love and intention. This hands-on approach allows couples to personalize the flavor and design and invest in the baking process with shared joy and anticipation.

Alternatively, collaborating with a skilled baker or confectioner will enable couples to bring their vision to life with professional expertise, ensuring that the peppermint wedding cookies are delicious and impeccably crafted.

Peppermint wedding cookies can serve as thoughtful and practical wedding favors for couples hosting destination weddings or intimate gatherings. The cookies are easy to transport, and their non-perishable nature ensures they remain fresh for an extended period. Couples may place the cookies in elegant gift boxes or organza bags, allowing guests to take home a sweet remembrance of the celebration. The portability and longevity of peppermint wedding cookies make them a versatile choice for various wedding settings, from beachside ceremonies to rustic countryside affairs.

Incorporating peppermint wedding cookies into wedding festivities extends beyond the act of gifting. Couples may integrate the cookies into the dessert spread, creating a thematic and cohesive culinary experience for their guests. Placing the cookies on a dedicated dessert table or incorporating them into the wedding cake display adds a visual element that complements the overall aesthetic. The cookies can be arranged in tiers, creating a stunning centerpiece that becomes a focal point of the celebration. The strategic placement of peppermint wedding cookies within the broader context of the wedding desserts enhances the overall sensory experience, ensuring that guests are treated to a delightful and memorable culinary journey.

As a versatile and customizable wedding favor, peppermint wedding cookies offer a charming and delectable way for couples to express gratitude to their guests. The choice of peppermint as a theme, with its festive flavors and symbolic significance, adds layers of meaning to the act of gifting. From the visual appeal and flavor profiles to creative presentations and personalized touches, peppermint wedding cookies become more than just sweet treats—they become an integral part of the love story that unfolds on the wedding day. In the sweet symphony of love and celebration, peppermint wedding cookies play a delightful and meaningful note, leaving a lasting impression on all who partake in the joyous occasion.

Hosting a Peppermint-Themed Holiday Party

As the winter season unfolds, a magical air sweeps through the air, heralding the arrival of holidays and festivities. One delightful way to embrace the season's spirit is by hosting a peppermint-themed holiday party. These gathering promises warmth and merriment and a symphony of flavors that capture the essence of winter. This essay explores the art of hosting a peppermint- themed holiday party, from the festive decorations and savory treats to the delectable array of peppermint- infused desserts, creating an enchanting winter wonderland for guests to savor and enjoy.

The foundation of any successful holiday party lies in

creating a festive atmosphere that immerses guests in the joyous spirit of the season. Hosting a peppermint-themed celebration allows hosts to deck the halls with classic red and white décor reminiscent of candy canes and peppermint swirls. From tablecloths and napkins to banners and centerpieces, infusing the space with a peppermint color palette sets the stage for a visually stunning and cohesive party experience. Adding twinkling lights, snowflake ornaments, and seasonal greenery further enhances the winter wonderland ambiance, creating a space that transports guests to enchantment and celebration.

The scent of peppermint becomes a sensory element that contributes to the overall atmosphere of the party.

Hosting a peppermint-themed holiday party invites hosts to infuse the air with peppermint's crisp and refreshing aroma. Scented candles, diffusers, or even simple bowls of peppermint-scented potpourri add a delightful olfactory dimension to the festivities, enveloping guests in the comforting fragrance of winter. The subtle infusion of peppermint scent becomes a subtle yet powerful element that enhances the overall ambiance, evoking feelings of nostalgia and seasonal joy.

As hosts set the stage for a peppermint-themed holiday party, attention to detail in the table settings adds more sophistication to the celebration. Combining red and white table linens, complemented by peppermint-striped napkin rings or elegant place card holders, creates a polished and cohesive look. Peppermint-themed dinnerware, such as plates and mugs adorned with festive designs, adds a touch of whimsy to the table. The thoughtful coordination of table settings allows hosts to create a visually appealing tableau that reflects the theme and elevates the dining experience for guests.

The culinary offerings at a peppermint-themed holiday party become a culinary journey through the flavors of winter. To begin the festivities, savory appetizers incorporating peppermint-infused elements set the tone for the evening. Peppermint-spiked cocktails or mocktails, served in festive glassware with candy cane stirrers, become a refreshing and thematic way to welcome guests. For a savory twist, appetizers like peppermint-infused bruschetta, goat cheese truffles with crushed peppermint coating, or even peppermint shrimp skewers offer a sophisticated and unexpected culinary experience.

Moving to the main course, hosts can continue to weave peppermint into the menu with creative and elegant dishes. Peppermint-glazed ham, roasted root vegetables with a hint of peppermint, or even peppermint-infused sauces add flavor to the meal. The key is to balance peppermint's savory and refreshing notes, creating a cohesive and delectable dining experience for guests. As hosts curate the menu, they consider dietary preferences and restrictions to ensure everyone can partake in the festive feast.

No holiday party is complete without a decadent array of desserts, and a peppermint-themed celebration offers the perfect opportunity to showcase a diverse selection of sweet treats. Peppermint bark, a classic confection of layered chocolate and peppermint, becomes a delightful centerpiece that captures the essence of the theme. Including peppermint-flavored cookies, cupcakes, and truffles adds variety to the dessert spread, allowing guests to indulge in various flavors and textures. For a show-stopping finale, a peppermint-inspired cake or a tiered dessert display featuring an array of mini peppermint delights becomes a visual and gustatory delight that leaves a lasting impression.

The art of incorporating peppermint into desserts extends beyond traditional confections to include creative and unexpected treats. Peppermint-flavored ice cream, sorbet, or gelato provides a refreshing and palate-cleansing option for those who prefer a lighter finish to the meal. Peppermint affogato, featuring a scoop of vanilla ice cream drowned in hot peppermint-infused espresso, offers a sophisticated and caffeinated twist. The versatility of peppermint as a flavor allows hosts to experiment with a wide range of desserts, ensuring that there's something for every palate.

In addition to the traditional peppermint desserts, hosting a peppermint-themed holiday party invites hosts to explore unique and innovative creations. Peppermint-infused panna cotta with a dark chocolate drizzle, peppermint mousse-filled chocolate cups, or even peppermint crème brûlée become elegant and unexpected options that elevate the dessert experience.

Incorporating diverse textures and presentation styles adds a layer of sophistication to the sweet offerings, creating a dessert spread that is as visually appealing as delectable.

Hosts may consider setting up a peppermint hot cocoa bar for a playful and interactive element. A spread of hot cocoa or hot chocolate, accompanied by peppermint-flavored syrups, whipped cream, marshmallows, and crushed peppermint toppings, allows guests to customize their warm beverages. The aroma of steaming cocoa infused with peppermint wafts through the air, creating a cozy and inviting atmosphere that encourages guests to linger and savor the moment.

The incorporation of peppermint extends beyond the culinary realm to include creative and engaging activities that enhance the overall experience of the party. Hosting a peppermint-scented crafting station, where guests can create their own peppermint-scented candles or potpourri sachets, adds a tactile and personalized element to the celebration. Alternatively, organizing a peppermint-themed game night with activities such as peppermint bingo, candy cane scavenger hunts, or even a peppermint-inspired version of charades infuses the party with laughter and camaraderie.

Music becomes an integral part of the festivities, and a carefully curated playlist featuring holiday classics and peppermint-themed tunes adds an auditory dimension to the party. From timeless melodies to contemporary peppermint-inspired tracks, the music sets the mood and encourages guests to embrace the joyous spirit of the season. For those who enjoy a live musical experience, hiring a local caroling group or even a jazz ensemble to perform peppermint-themed tunes adds a touch of live entertainment that elevates the party atmosphere.

The exchange of gifts becomes a cherished tradition during the holidays, and a peppermint-themed holiday

party provides the perfect opportunity for a festive gift exchange. Guests may bring peppermint-inspired gifts, such as scented candles, peppermint-flavored chocolates, or even handmade peppermint-infused bath salts. Exchanging gifts becomes a gesture of warmth and generosity, creating a shared joy and celebration among friends and loved ones.

As the party winds down, sending guests home with peppermint-themed party favors becomes a thoughtful and memorable gesture. Individual bags of homemade peppermint bark, personalized peppermint-scented candles, or even peppermint-flavored lip balm become delightful tokens that extend the spirit of the celebration beyond the party venue. Gifting peppermint-themed favors allows hosts to express gratitude to their guests and leave them a sweet reminder of the enchanting evening.

In conclusion, hosting a peppermint-themed holiday party is a delightful and creative way to celebrate the winter season with friends and loved ones. From the festive decorations and savory treats to the delectable array of peppermint-infused desserts, every element of the party contributes to creating a winter wonderland of flavor and festivity. The art of hosting a peppermint-themed holiday party lies in the thoughtful coordination of décor, culinary offerings, and engaging activities, creating an immersive and joyous experience for guests. As the air is filled with the crisp scent of peppermint and the sounds of laughter and merriment, the peppermint-themed holiday party becomes a cherished tradition that brings people together to savor the season's magic.

Homemade Peppermint Gift Baskets

Giving takes on a special significance in the spirit of the holiday season. Homemade peppermint gift baskets

emerge as a heartfelt and creative way to share the season's joy with friends, family, and loved ones. These thoughtfully curated baskets go beyond traditional presents, offering a personalized touch that reflects the warmth and festivity of the holidays. This essay delves into the art of creating homemade peppermint gift baskets, exploring the elements that make them unique, the variety of contents that can be included, and the joy they bring to both the giver and the recipient.

At the heart of homemade peppermint gift baskets is the intention to spread joy and create a memorable experience for the recipient. Crafting a personalized gift basket reflects the thought and care invested in selecting items that resonate with the recipient's tastes and preferences. With its crisp and invigorating aroma, Peppermint becomes a central theme that infuses the gift basket with the season's essence. The carefully chosen contents and the attention to detail in the presentation transform the gift-giving experience into a gesture of love and celebration.

The first step in creating homemade peppermint gift baskets is selecting a suitable container. Baskets, decorative boxes, or even reusable tote bags become vessels for holding the festive treasures within. The choice of container sets the tone for the overall aesthetic, allowing the giver to express their creativity and align the presentation with the theme of the holiday season. For those who prefer an eco-friendly approach, opting for reusable and sustainable containers adds a layer of thoughtfulness to the gift.

Peppermint becomes the gift basket's guiding star, and including peppermint-infused treats is a natural starting point. Classic peppermint bark, with its rich chocolate and refreshing peppermint layers, takes center stage as a quintessential holiday delight. Peppermint-flavored chocolates, candies, or even homemade peppermint

marshmallows add variety to the sweet offerings, creating a diverse and delightful assortment. The key is to strike a balance between the traditional and the unexpected, ensuring that each peppermint treat brings a sense of joy and anticipation.

Beyond sweets, homemade peppermint gift baskets offer the opportunity to incorporate various festive and practical items. Peppermint-scented candles, bath salts, or even scented sachets infuse the basket with the crisp aroma of winter. Including a cozy peppermint-scented blanket, a set of festive mugs, or even a charming ornament adds a touch of warmth and charm. The variety of items allows the giver to tailor the gift basket to the recipient's preferences, creating a truly personalized and meaningful present.

For those who enjoy a touch of DIY creativity, crafting homemade peppermint-themed items adds a special and unique dimension to the gift basket. Handmade peppermint sugar scrub, lip balm, or peppermint-infused potpourri become labor-of-love additions that showcase the giver's thoughtfulness and dedication. Including a handwritten recipe for peppermint hot cocoa or a peppermint-infused cocktail adds a personal touch, inviting the recipient to recreate the festive flavors at home. Incorporating homemade items transforms the gift basket into a curated collection of handmade treasures, adding an extra layer of intimacy to the gesture.

The presentation of homemade peppermint gift baskets is an art in itself. Attention to detail in arranging the contents, selecting complementary colors, and incorporating festive embellishments contribute to the overall visual appeal. Tying the basket with a vibrant peppermint-striped ribbon or adorning it with a personalized gift tag adds a finishing touch that elevates the presentation. The goal is to create a visually stunning and inviting gift that captivates the recipient from the moment they see it.

Giving homemade peppermint gift baskets becomes an opportunity to communicate warmth, love, and celebration. The contents of the basket, carefully selected and thoughtfully arranged, convey a message of joy and appreciation. Whether the gift is for a family member, a friend, or a colleague, the homemade nature of the basket adds an extra layer of sincerity and authenticity. In a world filled with commercialized products, a homemade gift basket stands out as a genuine expression of care and consideration.

Homemade peppermint gift baskets are versatile and can be tailored to suit a variety of occasions. Whether presented as a Christmas gift, a hostess present for a holiday gathering, or a festive birthday surprise, the gift baskets adapt to the theme of the celebration. The flexibility of the contents allows givers to customize the basket based on the recipient's preferences and the specific occasion, creating a personal and appropriate gift. Incorporating a theme within the gift basket adds an extra layer of cohesion and thoughtfulness. For example, a "Peppermint Spa Retreat" theme may include peppermint-scented bath salts, candles, and a cozy robe, creating an indulgent experience for the recipient. A "Peppermint Cozy Night In" theme may feature a peppermint hot cocoa mix, a festive mug, and a cozy blanket, inviting the recipient to unwind and savor the season's flavors. By incorporating a theme, givers can tailor the gift basket to create a curated experience that resonates with the recipient's lifestyle and preferences. The

joy of giving homemade peppermint gift baskets extends beyond the moment of exchange. The thoughtful curation and presentation of the basket create a lasting memory for both the giver and the recipient. The act of receiving a homemade gift basket invites the recipient to embark on a sensory journey, savoring each item and appreciating the effort and care that went into its creation. The basket becomes a source of delight, invoking a sense of celebration and warmth each time the recipient interacts with its contents.

For those who enjoy the art of gift-giving, creating a tradition of exchanging homemade peppermint gift baskets can add a meaningful and festive touch to the holiday season. Exchanging baskets with friends or family becomes a shared experience, fostering a sense of connection and joy. Each basket reflects the giver's personality and creativity, creating a delightful exchange that deepens the bonds of friendship and family.

Homemade peppermint gift baskets also allow givers to support local artisans and businesses. Including handmade peppermint treats, artisanal candles, or locally crafted items adds a layer of community engagement to the gift. Supporting local creators contributes to the community's vitality. It ensures that the gift basket is filled with unique, high-quality items that cannot be found in mass-produced alternatives. Gifting becomes a celebration of local talent and craftsmanship, infusing the basket with authenticity and character.

In conclusion, homemade peppermint gift baskets embody the spirit of the holiday season by offering a thoughtful and personal way to share joy with others. Carefully curating peppermint-infused treats, festive items, and handmade treasures creates a gift beyond material value, conveying a message of warmth and celebration. Giving homemade peppermint gift baskets becomes a joyful tradition that enhances the holiday experience for both the giver and the recipient, creating cherished memories that linger long after the season has passed.

CHAPTER X

Health-Conscious Peppermint Alternatives

Exploring Lighter Peppermint Options

With its invigorating and refreshing flavor, Peppermint has long been a staple in the world of confectionery and culinary delights. From candies to desserts, this versatile herb has found its way into various food products, becoming a beloved addition to many recipes. However, as the demand for healthier and lighter options continues to rise, the exploration of lighter peppermint alternatives has become a significant area of interest for consumers and producers alike.

The quest for reduced sugar content lies at the heart of the peppermint exploration. While delightful to the taste buds, traditional peppermint treats often come with a high sugar load that can be detrimental to one's health. Food scientists and manufacturers are working diligently to develop lighter peppermint options that deliver the same satisfaction without compromising taste in response to the growing awareness of the adverse effects of excessive sugar consumption.

One avenue of exploration involves using natural sweeteners as substitutes for refined sugars. Stevia, a plant-derived sweetener, has gained popularity recently due to its ability to impart sweetness without the caloric baggage associated with traditional sugars. Incorporating stevia into peppermint-flavored products allows for creating treats that cater to the health-conscious consumer, providing a guilt-free indulgence that doesn't compromise on the refreshing taste of peppermint.

Furthermore, the quest for lighter peppermint options extends beyond just sugar reduction. Alternative flours, such as almond flour or coconut flour, introduce a gluten-free element to peppermint-based recipes. This is particularly relevant as gluten-free diets become more prevalent, driven by both medical necessity and lifestyle choices. Gluten-free peppermint cookies or cakes offer a solution for those with dietary restrictions, ensuring that a wider audience can enjoy the joy of peppermint-infused treats.

In addition to addressing dietary concerns, exploring lighter peppermint options extends to beverages. Peppermint tea, renowned for its soothing properties, has become famous for those seeking a more lightweight alternative to sugary drinks. The infusion of peppermint leaves in hot water imparts a refreshing flavor and offers various health benefits, including improved digestion and stress relief. As consumers increasingly turn to beverages that contribute to their overall well-being, peppermint tea emerges as a natural and lighter option.

The incorporation of peppermint into health-focused products extends beyond the realms of food and beverages. Peppermint-scented personal care items like toothpaste and lip balm offer a lighter and more natural alternative to their artificially flavored counterparts. The refreshing aroma of peppermint adds a sensory element to these products, enhancing the overall user experience while avoiding the need for excessive artificial additives. Moreover, the exploration of lighter peppermint options aligns with the broader sustainability trend in the food industry. Sustainable practices, such as sourcing peppermint from local and eco-friendly farms, reduce environmental impact. By opting for lighter peppermint options that prioritize sustainability, consumers can make choices that benefit their health and support ethical and environmentally conscious practices within the industry.

The cultural significance of peppermint further enhances the appeal of exploring lighter options. Peppermint has a long history of being associated with festive occasions, particularly during the winter holiday season. More delicate peppermint treats, whether in candies, cookies, or beverages, allow individuals to partake in these cultural traditions without the excess baggage of unhealthy ingredients. As communities become more health-conscious, the demand for lighter peppermint options during celebratory periods continues to rise.

The culinary landscape is continually evolving, and the exploration of lighter peppermint options is a testament to the adaptability of the food industry. Consumers are no longer willing to compromise taste for health or vice versa. Instead, they seek a harmonious balance that allows for enjoying familiar flavors without the guilt associated with indulgence. The ongoing research and development in lighter peppermint options cater to this demand, providing consumers with a spectrum of choices that align with their evolving preferences and priorities.

In conclusion, exploring lighter peppermint options represents a dynamic and multifaceted journey within the food industry. From addressing health concerns to embracing sustainability and cultural significance, the quest for lighter peppermint alternatives reflects the industry's commitment to meeting the diverse needs of consumers. As science, technology, and culinary creativity converge, the future of peppermint-infused delights appears promising, offering a lighter and healthier palette for the enjoyment of all.

Moderation and Mindful Indulgence

In our fast-paced and often demanding world, pursuing a balanced and healthy lifestyle has become an increasingly prevalent goal. Among the myriad wellness strategies, the principles of moderation and mindful indulgence stand out as guiding lights, offering individuals a nuanced approach to physical and mental well-being. These concepts underscore the importance of avoiding extremes and fostering a sustainable and enjoyable way of living that doesn't compromise on the richness of experience.

At moderation's core is finding a middle ground – a space between excess and deprivation. This principle transcends various aspects of life, from dietary habits to work-life balance. In nutrition, moderation encourages a sensible approach to eating, steering individuals away from the pitfalls of overindulgence or restrictive diets. The concept acknowledges that the enjoyment of food is an integral part of the human experience and that denying oneself culinary pleasures can lead to an unsustainable and joyless approach to nutrition.

Mindful indulgence complements moderation by emphasizing the importance of being fully present in the moment, particularly when engaging in pleasurable activities. Instead of mindlessly consuming, whether it be food, entertainment, or experiences, the practice of mindful indulgence encourages individuals to savor and appreciate each moment. This enhances the overall experience and fosters a deeper connection with one's surroundings and emotions.

Regarding dietary habits, the synergy between moderation and mindful indulgence becomes evident.

Rather than adhering to restrictive diets that categorize foods as strictly "good" or "bad," individuals can adopt a more balanced and flexible approach. This allows for enjoying diverse foods while being mindful of portion sizes and nutritional content. By savoring each bite and paying attention to hunger and satiety cues, individuals can cultivate a healthier relationship with food, one that is sustainable in the long term.

The principles of moderation and mindful indulgence extend beyond the dining table, permeating various facets of life. In the context of physical activity, moderation promotes a realistic and sustainable approach to exercise. Striking a balance between rest and activity is crucial for overall well-being, preventing burnout, and mitigating the risk of injury. Mindful indulgence in physical activities involves choosing forms of exercise that bring joy and fulfillment rather than adhering to punishing routines solely for the sake of meeting fitness goals.

The workplace is another arena where moderation and mindful indulgence are beneficial. In a society driven by productivity, individuals often find themselves caught in the perpetual pursuit of professional success at the expense of their well-being. Embracing moderation in work commitments involves setting realistic goals and boundaries and recognizing the importance of rest and leisure. In this context, mindful indulgence encourages individuals to immerse themselves fully in their work when necessary but also to step back and recharge when the demands become overwhelming.

The link between mental health, moderation principles, and mindful indulgence is profound. In an age of constant connectivity and information overload, moderation in digital content consumption becomes essential. Excessive screen time and social media engagement can contribute to stress and anxiety. Mindful indulgence encourages individuals to cultivate digital habits that enhance well-being, such as engaging in purposeful online activities and taking breaks to foster mindfulness and relaxation.

Furthermore, moderation and mindful indulgence are pivotal in managing stress and emotional well-being. Moderation involves acknowledging and addressing stressors measuredly, avoiding the pitfalls of either neglecting or obsessing over them. On the other hand, mindful indulgence encourages exploring activities that bring joy and relaxation, whether through hobbies, socializing, or simply taking time for oneself. These practices contribute to a resilient and adaptive mindset, enabling individuals to navigate life's challenges with more excellent balance.

In relationships, the principles of moderation and mindful indulgence are equally relevant. Striking a balance between personal and social commitments is crucial for maintaining healthy connections. Moderation encourages individuals to assess their time and energy demands, ensuring that relationships contribute positively to their well-being without becoming overwhelming. Mindful indulgence in relationships involves being fully present and engaged during interactions, fostering genuine connections rather than superficial engagements driven by obligation.

As individuals embrace the principles of moderation and mindful indulgence, they shift how they approach and perceive their lives. The constant pressure to conform to societal expectations gives way to a more authentic and intentional way of living. This shift is not about adopting a rigid set of rules but rather about cultivating self-awareness and making choices that align with one's values and priorities.

In the culinary realm, for instance, moderation and mindful indulgence can reshape how individuals view food. Instead of viewing certain foods as forbidden or indulging in them recklessly, individuals can approach eating with a sense of mindfulness. This involves savoring flavors, appreciating the effort in preparing a meal and being attuned to how food makes them feel physically and emotionally. The result is a more harmonious relationship with food, transcending the dichotomy of guilt and pleasure.

The principles of moderation and mindful indulgence also extend to the broader environmental and societal context. In an era where excess consumption contributes to ecological challenges, adopting moderation becomes a form of responsible stewardship. Mindful indulgence in this context involves making choices that align with sustainable practices, from conscious shopping and reducing waste to supporting eco-friendly initiatives. Individuals can contribute to a more balanced and sustainable world by incorporating these principles into lifestyle choices.

In conclusion, moderation and mindful indulgence emerge as guiding principles that facilitate a balanced and fulfilling approach to life. From dietary habits to work, relationships, and the broader societal context, these principles offer a roadmap for navigating the complexities of modern existence. As individuals embrace the synergy between moderation and mindful indulgence, they discover a path that prioritizes well-being, authenticity, and a deeper connection with the richness of the human experience. In this balanced approach to living, individuals find physical health and a profound sense of fulfillment and contentment.

Sharing the Joy of Healthy Peppermint

With its invigorating and refreshing flavor, Peppermint has transcended traditional confectionery to become a symbol of culinary delight and festivity. As a beloved herb, peppermint has found its way into various delectable treats, from candies and desserts to beverages and savory dishes. However, in the contemporary landscape where health-conscious choices dominate, the exploration of healthy peppermint options has become a culinary adventure that seeks to share the joy of this versatile herb while aligning with modern wellness priorities.

At the forefront of the quest for healthier peppermint options is the desire to minimize the reliance on refined sugars. The traditional peppermint treats that grace holiday tables are often laden with sugar, contributing to concerns about excessive calorie intake and its associated health risks. In response to these concerns, culinary enthusiasts and health-conscious chefs are experimenting with alternative sweeteners that allow for the creation of healthier, yet equally delightful, peppermint-infused delicacies. Stevia, a natural sweetener derived from the leaves of the Stevia rebaudiana plant, has gained popularity as a substitute for sugar in peppermint recipes. This substitution reduces the calorie content of the treats and caters to individuals with dietary restrictions, such as those managing diabetes or aiming to minimize their sugar intake.

The pursuit of healthy peppermint options also extends to the realm of flours. Traditional recipes often rely on refined flours, which may not align with the preferences of those following gluten-free or low-carb diets. Almond flour and coconut flour have emerged as wholesome alternatives that contribute unique textures to peppermint treats and cater to a broader spectrum of dietary needs. Gluten-free peppermint cookies and cakes, made with these alternative flours, provide a guilt-free indulgence for those with gluten sensitivities, allowing them to partake in the joy of peppermint-infused delights without compromising their dietary choices.

Beyond the consideration of sweet treats, incorporating peppermint into beverages has become a focal point in the quest for healthier options. Peppermint tea, celebrated for its soothing properties, stands out as a beacon of health-conscious refreshment. The infusion of peppermint leaves into hot water imparts a delightful flavor and offers many health benefits, including digestive support and stress relief. As individuals increasingly seek beverages that contribute positively to their well-being, peppermint tea emerges as a beacon of taste and health, fostering a shared joy in sipping on a beverage that is as revitalizing as beneficial.

Furthermore, the joy of healthy peppermint transcends the boundaries of the kitchen and extends to personal care products. Peppermint-infused toothpaste and lip balm have become staples in the pursuit of oral hygiene and sensory delight. The refreshing and cooling properties of peppermint add an extra layer of joy to everyday routines, transforming mundane activities into sensory experiences. Sharing the joy of healthy peppermint through personal care products is a testament to the versatility of this herb, offering individuals a holistic approach to well-being beyond culinary delights.

As the culinary landscape evolves, exploring healthy peppermint options aligns with the broader sustainability trend. Sourcing peppermint from local and eco-friendly farms becomes a priority, contributing to reduced environmental impact and supporting ethical agricultural practices. By embracing sustainable sourcing, culinary enthusiasts and chefs enhance the nutritional value of their creations and contribute to the planet's well-being, sharing the joy of peppermint in an environmentally responsible way.

The cultural significance of peppermint further amplifies the joy of incorporating it into healthy culinary creations. Peppermint has long been associated with festive occasions, particularly during the winter holiday season. By infusing a health-conscious approach into traditional peppermint recipes, individuals can share the joy of these festive treats without the guilt associated with excessive sugar and unhealthy ingredients. Sharing healthier peppermint options during celebrations becomes a way to honor cultural traditions while embracing modern sensibilities.

In the realm of community and social connection, the joy of healthy peppermint takes on a communal dimension. Cooking classes, workshops, and community events centered around creating and sharing healthy peppermint-infused recipes foster a sense of togetherness and shared joy. These gatherings become spaces for culinary exploration, learning, and exchanging ideas, creating a ripple effect that extends beyond the kitchen and into the broader community. The joy of healthy peppermint becomes a catalyst for strengthening social bonds and promoting collective well-being.

Moreover, digital platforms and social media have facilitated the global sharing of healthy peppermint recipes. Food bloggers, chefs, and home cooks contribute to a virtual tapestry of culinary creativity, inspiring others to join the journey of crafting and sharing health-conscious peppermint delights. The joy of healthy peppermint becomes a shared experience that transcends geographical boundaries, connecting individuals worldwide through a shared appreciation for culinary artistry and mindful well-being.

In conclusion, exploring healthy peppermint options represents a culinary adventure beyond the confines of the kitchen. It is a journey infused with the joy of creating and sharing delightful treats that align with modern wellness priorities. From reducing sugar content to incorporating alternative flours, peppermint tea, and sustainable sourcing, the quest for healthy peppermint options is a dynamic and evolving exploration of culinary possibilities. As individuals, communities, and cultures embrace this journey, the joy of beneficial peppermint becomes a shared celebration of a global culinary community's flavor, well-being, and interconnectedness.

CHAPTER XI

Healthier Twists on Peppermint Delights

Oat Flour Peppermint Protein Cookies

In the realm of festive baking, the fusion of health-conscious choices and indulgent flavors has become increasingly popular. One delightful manifestation of this trend is the creation of "Oat Flour Peppermint Protein Cookies." These cookies capture the essence of the holiday season with the refreshing taste of peppermint and offer a nutritious twist by incorporating oat flour and protein-rich ingredients.

The foundation of these cookies lies in the choice of oat flour as a primary ingredient. Oat flour, derived from ground oats, brings a distinct nutty flavor and a hearty texture to the cookies. Beyond its rich taste, oat flour is a versatile and healthier alternative to all-purpose flour. It boasts a higher fiber content, promoting satiety and aiding in digestive health. Additionally, oat flour is a good source of complex carbohydrates, providing a sustained release of energy—making it an ideal choice for those seeking a nourishing treat without compromising taste.

Peppermint, a quintessential holiday season flavor, takes center stage in these cookies, imparting a burst of freshness and a delightful aroma. The combination of oat flour and peppermint creates a harmonious balance, with the earthiness of oats complementing the excellent, minty notes. This dynamic duo satisfies the sweet tooth and elevates the overall sensory experience, making these cookies a perfect addition to festive gatherings and cozy evenings by the fireplace.

Incorporating protein into these cookies adds a nutritional punch, making them a guilt-free indulgence. Protein is a macronutrient crucial to muscle repair, immune function, and overall well-being. By infusing these cookies with protein, they become a more substantial snack, offering a satiating option for those looking to satisfy hunger while enjoying a holiday treat. Ingredients such as protein powder, nut butter, or even Greek yogurt seamlessly integrate into the cookie dough, enhancing the texture and nutritional value.

Creating Oat Flour Peppermint Protein Cookies is not just about following a recipe; it's an invitation to explore variations and personalize the experience. Experimenting with different protein sources, such as whey, plant-based, or collagen, allows for customization based on dietary preferences. Nut butter like almond or peanut not only contributes to the protein content but also adds a creamy richness, enhancing the overall mouthfeel of the cookies. This adaptability ensures that these cookies can cater to diverse tastes and dietary requirements, making them an inclusive and crowd-pleasing option for holiday celebrations.

Furthermore, baking these cookies provides an opportunity to appreciate the artistry and mindfulness of the culinary craft. The careful measuring and blending of ingredients, the aroma that wafts through the kitchen as the cookies bake, and the anticipation of the first bite all contribute to a multisensory experience. Baking becomes a form of self-expression and a means of sharing love and joy. With their unique blend of wholesome ingredients and festive flavors, Oat Flour Peppermint Protein Cookies encapsulate the season's spirit and embody the joy of giving and savoring delightful moments.

In health-conscious baking, these cookies stand as a testament to the evolving landscape of culinary innovation. They debunk the myth that indulgence and nutrition are mutually exclusive, demonstrating that one can savor the pleasures of the holiday season without compromising on well-being. Oat Flour Peppermint Protein Cookies are more than a treat; they represent a mindful approach to celebrating, nourishing the body, and embracing the spirit of togetherness that defines the magic of the holidays. As we gather around tables adorned with these delectable creations, we not only indulge in a festive delight but also partake in a shared experience that transcends the boundaries of taste, embodying the warmth and joy of the season.

Paleo-Friendly Peppermint Crunch Bars

In the ever-evolving landscape of dietary preferences and health-conscious living, the Paleo diet has emerged as a popular choice for those seeking a more natural and ancestral approach to nutrition. Within Paleo-friendly desserts, one standout creation that embodies the essence of the holiday season is the "Paleo-Friendly Peppermint Crunch Bars." These bars seamlessly blend the principles of the Paleo diet with the festive allure of peppermint, offering a guilt-free indulgence that captures the spirit of celebration.

At the heart of these delectable bars lies the commitment to Paleo-friendly ingredients, avoiding grains, dairy, and refined sugars. Almond flour, a staple in Paleo baking, is the foundational element, imparting a nutty richness and a delicate crumb to the bars. This gluten-free alternative aligns with the Paleo ethos and contributes a wholesome texture that enhances the overall sensory experience. Coconut oil, another cornerstone of the Paleo diet, steps in to replace traditional butter, adding a subtle tropical note and ensuring a moist and decadent consistency.

Including peppermint in the Paleo-Friendly Peppermint Crunch Bars introduces a festive twist, evoking the timeless association of peppermint with the holiday season. The calm and refreshing flavor of peppermint creates a delightful contrast to the warmth of almond flour and coconut oil, resulting in a flavor profile that resonates with the comforting traditions of winter festivities. Peppermint, known for its aromatic qualities, infuses the bars with a refreshing aroma that tantalizes the senses, making each bite a journey into the heart of holiday cheer.

Crucial to the "crunch" aspect of these bars is incorporating Paleo-friendly nuts and seeds. Chopped almonds, walnuts, and sunflower seeds contribute to the robust texture and introduce a spectrum of nutty flavors. The combination of these crunchy elements elevates the bars, providing a satisfying contrast to the softness of the almond flour base. The Paleo-Friendly Peppermint Crunch Bars deliver a textural symphony that engages the palate, offering an enjoyable and wholesome crunch with every bite.

The sweetener in Paleo baking often comes from natural alternatives such as honey or maple syrup. In the case of these peppermint-infused bars, the sweetness of pure maple syrup takes center stage, enhancing the overall flavor profile without compromising the commitment to unrefined sweeteners. This choice aligns with the Paleo philosophy and imparts a nuanced sweetness that harmonizes with the other ingredients, creating a well-balanced and satisfying treat.

The process of crafting Paleo-Friendly Peppermint Crunch Bars is not merely a culinary endeavor; it is a celebration of creativity within the constraints of a specific dietary approach. It requires a thoughtful selection of ingredients that adhere to the principles of the Paleo diet while ensuring a harmonious fusion of flavors and textures. The artistry of Paleo baking lies in the ability to navigate the limitations and transform them into opportunities for culinary expression. In this context, the creation of these peppermint-infused bars becomes a testament to the ingenuity of Paleo baking—a delightful intersection of tradition, innovation, and mindful eating.

Beyond their delightful taste and adherence to dietary guidelines, these bars offer a nutritional profile that aligns with the broader goals of the Paleo lifestyle. Almond flour, rich in healthy fats and protein, provides sustained energy, making these bars a satiating snack. The inclusion of nuts and seeds not only contributes to the crunch but introduces an array of vitamins, minerals, and antioxidants. Coconut oil, with its medium-chain triglycerides, supports metabolic health, adding to the overall nutritional value of the bars. Thus, Paleo-Friendly Peppermint Crunch Bars are not just a momentary indulgence; they embody a commitment to nourishing the body with wholesome ingredients in a way that respects ancestral nutrition principles.

These Paleo-Friendly Peppermint Crunch Bars grace holiday dessert tables and carry a narrative of intentionality and conscientious choices. Sharing these treats becomes a gesture of consideration for diverse dietary needs, inviting everyone to partake in the joy of festive indulgence. The bars symbolize inclusivity, demonstrating that one can adhere to dietary preferences without sacrificing the enjoyment and flavor of holiday treats.

The Paleo-Friendly Peppermint Crunch Bars transcend their status as a dessert; they represent a mindful approach to culinary choices and a bridge between the joy of celebration and the commitment to well-being. As we savor each bite of these bars, we not only indulge in a delicious treat but also partake in a culinary journey that honors tradition, embraces innovation, and encapsulates the spirit of the holidays—a spirit that celebrates both the joy of indulgence and the wisdom of mindful eating.

Sugar-Free Peppermint Bliss Balls

In the quest for healthier and mindful eating, sugar-free alternatives have paved the way for a delightful yet guilt-free indulgence, exemplified by creations like "Sugar-Free Peppermint Bliss Balls." These bite-sized treats not only cater to the sweet tooth but also align with the growing awareness of the impact of refined sugars on overall health. Rooted in balanced nutrition and mindful consumption, Sugar-Free Peppermint Bliss Balls offer a compelling blend of flavors and textures without the need for traditional sugars.

At the heart of these bliss balls is the commitment to eliminating refined sugars, a significant departure from conventional sweet treats. Instead, the sweetness is derived from natural sources such as dates, stevia, or monk fruit sweeteners. This departure from refined sugars addresses concerns related to added sugars and their potential health implications. It creates a treat suitable for those with dietary restrictions, such as individuals managing diabetes or those seeking a low-glycemic alternative.

The choice of dates as a primary sweetener adds natural sweetness and contributes to the gooey and chewy texture that defines bliss balls. Dates are rich in fiber, vitamins, and minerals, providing a natural sweetening agent and a source of sustained energy. The synergy between the natural sugars in dates and the cooling essence of peppermint creates a harmonious flavor profile that captures the nature of the holiday season without compromising on nutritional integrity.

Peppermint, a timeless flavor associated with winter festivities, takes center stage in Sugar-Free Peppermint

Bliss Balls, offering a refreshing and invigorating twist. The calm and minty notes of peppermint not only stimulate the senses but also provide a counterbalance to the sweetness of the dates. This dynamic interplay of flavors transforms each bite into a sensory experience, making these bliss balls a delightful and health-conscious alternative to traditional peppermint treats.

Including nuts and seeds further elevates the nutritional profile of Sugar-Free Peppermint Bliss Balls. Almonds, walnuts, or cashews contribute healthy fats, proteins, and a satisfying crunch. These ingredients enhance the texture and introduce a spectrum of essential nutrients, making each bliss ball a nutrient-dense snack. The combination of nuts, seeds, and peppermint creates a symphony of flavors that lingers on the palate, offering a well-rounded and satiating treat.

Crafting Sugar-Free Peppermint Bliss Balls involves a certain level of culinary artistry, as the balance of ingredients becomes crucial to achieving the desired texture and taste. Careful consideration is given to the choice of nuts, the proportion of peppermint, and the blending of dates to create a cohesive mixture. The art lies in achieving the right consistency that allows for easy shaping of the bliss balls while ensuring a pleasing mouthfeel with every bite.

These bliss balls transcend their status as a sweet treat; they embody a mindful and intentional eating philosophy. The absence of refined sugars aligns with the broader movement towards reducing added sugars in the diet, acknowledging the impact of excessive sugar consumption on health. Sugar-Free Peppermint Bliss Balls become a conscious choice, an invitation to savor the sweetness of natural ingredients while being mindful of overall well-being.

Moreover, the portability and convenience of Sugar-Free Peppermint Bliss Balls make them a practical and nutritious snack for individuals leading busy lives. These bliss balls cater to various occasions, whether tucked into a lunchbox, enjoyed as a mid-afternoon pick-me-up, or served as a guilt-free dessert at festive gatherings. Their bite-sized nature encourages mindful portion control, allowing for a sweet treat without worrying about excess sugars, a common concern in health-conscious eating.

As these bliss balls grace holiday tables, they represent a departure from the conventional notion that indulgence must come at the cost of health. They become a symbol of balance, embodying the idea that pleasure and nourishment can coexist. The joy derived from savoring these treats extends beyond the momentary sweetness; it encapsulates the satisfaction of making informed choices that contribute to overall well-being.

In the broader context of dietary awareness, Sugar-Free Peppermint Bliss Balls contribute to a paradigm shift in how we perceive and consume sweets. They challenge the notion that sweetness is synonymous with refined sugars, presenting a delicious alternative that champions the inherent sweetness of natural ingredients. This paradigm shift reflects a cultural evolution—a growing consciousness that seeks to redefine our relationship with food, emphasizing quality, balance, and the holistic impact on health.

In conclusion, Sugar-Free Peppermint Bliss Balls are a testament to the evolving landscape of culinary creativity and mindful eating. They encapsulate the joy of the holiday season while embodying a commitment to health-conscious choices. As we indulge in these bite-sized delights, we savor the peppermint-infused sweetness and partake in a broader narrative that celebrates the fusion of flavor, nutrition, and intentionality. These bliss balls manifest the belief that sweetness can be savored without compromise and that the journey towards a healthier and more conscious eating approach is blissful.

CONCLUSION

In conclusion, "Peppermint Perfection in Holiday Cookies: Candy Cane-Inspired Treats" encapsulates the essence of festive culinary delights, offering a delightful journey into the world of peppermint-infused confections. This e-book is a collection of recipes and a celebration of the joy, tradition, and creativity associated with holiday baking. By focusing on peppermint's versatile and refreshing flavor, the e-book provides both novice and seasoned bakers with a curated selection of recipes that evoke the warmth and spirit of the holiday season.

The e-book's emphasis on peppermint perfection extends beyond the traditional boundaries of holiday treats. It explores healthier alternatives, showcasing a mindful approach to indulgence that aligns with contemporary wellness trends. Incorporating natural sweeteners, alternative flours, and sustainable sourcing reflects a commitment to flavor and well-being, ensuring that the joy of peppermint is experienced without compromising on health-conscious choices.

One of the e-book's notable strengths lies in its ability to cater to a diverse audience. It welcomes individuals seeking classic holiday cookies with a peppermint twist or those interested in exploring gluten-free and low-sugar options. This inclusivity makes it a valuable resource for those navigating the complex landscape of holiday baking in a health-conscious era.

Furthermore, the e-book fosters community by encouraging readers to share their experiences and creations. Including tips, variations, and anecdotes enhances the user experience and transforms the e-book into a communal space where bakers can connect, exchange ideas, and celebrate their culinary achievements. In this way, "Peppermint Perfection in

Holiday Cookies: Candy Cane-Inspired Treats" goes beyond being a mere recipe compilation; it becomes a platform for shared enthusiasm and creativity.

As readers embark on their peppermint-inspired baking adventures, the e-book serves as a reliable guide, offering step-by-step instructions and insights into the cultural and festive significance of peppermint. The connection between tradition and innovation is masterfully woven throughout the e-book, allowing bakers to honor time-honored holiday customs while embracing contemporary culinary approaches.

In essence, "Peppermint Perfection in Holiday Cookies: Candy Cane-Inspired Treats" is more than a cookbook; it is an invitation to partake in the joyous tradition of holiday baking infused with the refreshing spirit of peppermint. Through its thoughtful curation, health-conscious exploration, and community-building elements, the e-book leaves a lasting impression, inspiring individuals to not only savor the delicious treats within its pages but also to create enduring memories and traditions that echo the festive cheer embodied in every peppermint-infused cookie.

Thank you for buying and reading/ listening to our book. If you found this book useful/ helpful please take a few minutes and leave a review on the platform where you purchased our book. Your feedback matters greatly to us.

www.ingramcontent.com/pod-product-compliance
Lightning Source LLC
Chambersburg PA
CBHW071526150726
48000CB00002B/699